bird on a wire

bird on a wire

Theresa Gattung
The Inside Story from a Straight-talking CEO

RANDOM HOUSE
NEW ZEALAND

A RANDOM HOUSE BOOK published by Random House New Zealand
18 Poland Road, Glenfield, Auckland, New Zealand

For more information about our titles go to www.randomhouse.co.nz

A catalogue record for this book is available from the National Library of New Zealand

Random House New Zealand is part of the Random House Group
New York   London   Sydney   Auckland   Delhi   Johannesburg

First published 2010. Reprinted 2010.

ISBN 978 1 86979 294 7

Cover images: Jane Ussher
Wool jacket by Alison Blain and blouse by Trelise Cooper. Citrine necklace by Alison
Blain.

Design: Laura Forlong
Printed in New Zealand by McCollams

Acknowledgements

No one finishes a book and says 'Gosh, that was easier than I thought it would be'. And so it has been with me. It's been fascinating, though, excavating past, present and future. This book is in large part a memoir, partly but not totally based on diaries I kept over the years. Some events covered are a matter of record; the rest is my interpretation of events.

There are some special people I'd like to thank.

First, Nicola Legat, publishing director at Random House. As a first-time author who didn't have a very good idea of what she was getting herself into, I found it a pleasure to work with you.

My darling sister Angela, who really is of the angels — thank you for helping me catalogue my voluminous source material.

John Savage, my former partner and forever friend — thank you for helping me with some of the original research drawn upon in the second half of the book, and for being big enough to be comfortable with me talking about what happened in our relationship.

My dear, dear friend Margaret Doucas — thank you for being a constant source of support during the writing of this book.

And finally to my closest friends who reviewed drafts for me — you know who you are and I love you all.

Theresa Gattung
Wellington
December 2009

Contents

a new direction

One crisp South Island evening in August 2009 I found myself in Oamaru, speaking to a group of about 70 businesswomen gathered at Portside restaurant. I am asked to speak to groups all the time and I generally decline, but when local businesswoman Sue Morton asked me to come and speak to her business network, it ticked three of my boxes: Will this advance the recovery of the wool industry in New Zealand? Will this inspire and motivate women as I, in turn, have been inspired and helped by the women who went before me? And, finally, is it somewhere I would like to go?

It turned out to be a wonderful evening, with the discussion ranging over many themes, from doing business in a recession to feminism. When we finished, I climbed into Cindy and David Douglas's four-wheel-drive for the 45-minute drive to their home at Dome Hills Station. On a property framed by mountains which are under snow for many months of the year, Cindy and David have diversified their business from pastoral farming to include tourism, and Cindy operates a tourist lodge on the station. However, she thought I might feel a bit isolated staying there by myself so she kindly offered me her daughter Lucy's bedroom to stay in, as Lucy was away at university. The next morning David, Cindy and I drove through the snow around the station and talked about sheep, skiing and land tenure review. It all felt a very long way from anything I'd ever done before.

It was the third iconic South Island high-country station I'd been on in eight weeks, after John and Heather Perriam's Bendigo Station in Central Otago, and Christine Fernyhough and John Bougen's Castle Hill Station in Canterbury. On Castle Hill I'd spent the afternoon mustering merinos with John Bougen and just one huntaway dog. At Bendigo, friends and I had enjoyed John Perriam's wonderful hospitality in his restored turn-of-the-century homestead and visited the adjacent gold-mining settlement remains.

These visits were part of a new venture for me, chairing Wool Partners International, a commercial entity set up to reinvigorate New Zealand's strong wool industry — that is, wool 28.5 microns or coarser, used primarily for carpets. This wool comes from sheep such as Romneys. We had just launched a premium brand, Laneve, and announced deals with two large US carpet manufacturers, Glen Eden Wool Carpet and Bellbridge Carpets, to manufacture Laneve ranges from early 2010. These recent milestones, the three high-country sheep station visits and the talks I had been giving to various rural groups, consolidated the feeling that I was in the thick of farming issues and that this was an exciting — and pivotal — time for both sheep farmers and the wool industry.

New Zealand was built on the sheep's back, as they say. Wool was once the country's major export, but this proud industry had been in decline for around 30 years, completely outmarketed internationally by the synthetic carpet industry and driven by acrimony, narrow self-interest and far too many players at home. During the previous 12 months, the chief executive of Wool Partners we had recruited, Iain Abercrombie, had taken on a rather heroic challenge: to convince farmers that there was a future for strong wool and demonstrate that the right strategy for success was to bring growers and the market much closer together than the current fragmented state. This was along similar lines to the successful model of New Zealand Merino Ltd, a company formed in the mid to late 1990s to market and promote merino — fine wool.

At my talk in Oamaru, and at Bendigo, Castle Hill and Dome Hills stations, the conversation quickly turned to the crisis facing sheep farmers today. Twenty years ago farmers were paid $6 a kilo for wool used in carpets, but by 2009 they were lucky to be getting half that. Manufacturers in the United States told us that the price of synthetic carpets, which are produced from oil, rose nine times in the year to July 2008, when the oil price hit US$150 a barrel, yet prices paid to sheep farmers for wool declined.

New Zealand produces 30 per cent of the strong wool traded worldwide. We also produce the highest quality wool in the world. This is not just a story we tell ourselves: when I went to the United States in late 2008 and listened to manufacturers big and small, they all said New Zealand wool was the best in the world. Despite this, there have been very poor returns to growers for at least two decades, and over that time our sheep population has dropped from well over 60 million to just over 30 million.

As we discussed that night in Oamaru, how many industries are there in which New Zealand has world-scale volume and a quality advantage? Not many. Perhaps only dairy, and look how the success of Fonterra, New Zealand's multibillion-dollar dairy cooperative, has transformed the agricultural sector to the benefit of farmers and all New Zealanders. We all agreed — wool should be a marketer's dream. Instead, the near disintegration of this industry is a national tragedy.

Nylon carpet was invented as a cheaper alternative to wool, but it has grown in popularity and now only a fraction of carpet sold in the United States is wool. Worse, the marketing of the nylon carpet industry features lambs — so they have outmarketed wool using wool's own imagery!

There have been many books written on the wool industry, and a useful place to start is the gradual demise of the New Zealand Wool Board, which began in the 1990s although formal disestablishment didn't occur until 2003. New Zealand started withdrawing from the International Wool Secretariat (IWS) in 1994. This meant New Zealand no longer had rights to use its Woolmark — a very well-recognised brand — and it was replaced by the Wools of New Zealand fern-frond identity, often referred to as the 'fern mark'. Farmers from those days tell me that New Zealand wool growers did not feel they were getting a fair shot from the IWS whose focus was much more on Australia.

With the industry in flux, New Zealand merino growers, who numbered only many hundreds rather than the many thousands of strong wool growers, seized the chance to do their own thing, setting up their own marketing organisation. Bendigo's John Perriam was a key player when New Zealand Merino was formed. Through the company working with the likes of clothing manufacturer Icebreaker in New Zealand and SmartWool in the United States, the price growers receive for merino has steadily risen. When New Zealand Merino started in 1996, 19-micron wool sold for $6.76 a kilo, around 15 per cent cheaper than Australian wool at that time. By late 2009 New Zealand Merino was offering 19-micron contracts for the active outdoor market at $14 a kilo — a premium of 18 per cent over average Australian prices since 1996. That turnaround was achieved by the growers partnering with manufacturers who produced great products and told the story behind them.

Wool is traditionally a very fragmented industry, with farmers often selling wool to brokers, who then sell it at auction for whatever the price is on the day. Of course, wool is not a disposable product. If a tanker doesn't turn up at a dairy farm to pick up the milk, the farmer's got a problem, but with wool, growers can choose when they shear, and how long to keep the wool before they sell it. There is some wool in storage in Napier that's been there for 18 years! Traders buy the wool at auction and sell it overseas, sometimes directly to manufacturers and sometimes to agents, who in turn sell it to manufacturers. No way is it a value chain: at best it's a supply chain, and a very inefficient one at that because unless you spin your own wool for knitting, you don't buy wool, you buy yarn. The whole process of collecting the wool, cleaning it, spinning it, weaving it and turning it into a finished product can take place through many different countries.

I believe that the formation of Wool Partners International is the solution that could turn the industry around. Our principles are to start with the market and create an integrated channel to reach it. We want to leverage New Zealand's current capabilities, built on 170 years of knowledge and research and development in wool, to collaborate within the industry, securing agreements with manufacturers and large end-user customers that will realise a premium for the quality of New Zealand's wool and will add value by having the wool spun here wherever possible. We will build on New Zealand's competitive advantages: our volume, our quality, our sustainability and our reputation. We want to unify New Zealand wool growers, consolidate the wool clip and innovate in the market. We strongly believe that unless farmers control their own industry it will not have a sustainable future, so Wool Partners was set up to be half-owned and majority controlled by the farmer cooperative Wool Grower Holdings, and half-owned by the New Zealand rural services supply company PGG Wrightson and we are very open to the participation of others.

In December 2008 we bought Wools of New Zealand, the company that owned the only international brand marketing support structure for New Zealand wool in the world, with more than 120 manufacturing partners worldwide. Wools of New Zealand was established in 1994 by the Wool Board and was an 'industry good' body funded by a levy on farmers, charging carpet manufacturers a few thousand dollars a year to use the brand on their carpet. But it wasn't able to sell wool directly because it wasn't a commercial company and didn't have any direct links with growers.

In the six months after buying Wools of New Zealand and developing our premium brand Laneve, we had a dozen agreements with manufacturers who wanted to be part of what we were trying to create — a strong market identity for New Zealand wool as a premium product.

My vision for the New Zealand wool industry is a combination of what Fonterra has done in terms of aggregating supply and creating a commercially driven organisation, and what New Zealand Merino has done in completely repositioning fine wool. Remember when we used to think wool was that scratchy thing you'd never wear next to your skin? We want to emulate with carpets the fashion component that is now intricately linked with fine merino clothing — after all, we're as likely to read magazines about decorating our homes as we are fashion magazines about decorating our bodies. Finally, we also want to take a leaf out of the wine industry's book by showcasing different varieties and regional variations. Different breeds of sheep not only have their own personalities, their wool also has different characteristics and is best used for different purposes. We want to reintroduce a luxury fibre to a changing world.

One of the first projects we took on in that first year was the creation of a premium marketing brand, similar to Cervena for export venison and Zespri for kiwifruit, and I enjoyed putting my skills to use in this context. We created the brand Laneve — a combination of *laneus*, the Latin word meaning woollen, and weave which nicely rolls off the tongue — which would stand alongside the brand names of the manufacturers. But Laneve isn't just a brand name: it will also stand for high-quality animal management practices, the quality of the product and its direct path to market.

The two contracts with American manufacturers — Glen Eden and Bellbridge — and the dozen other contracts with US manufacturers that have followed are just the first steps in what is going to be a multi-year recovery programme. And now we've also succeeded in getting wool back into the game in the green buildings code in the United States — so it is measured against its own set of criteria rather than compared to synthetics — I feel sure we are on the right track.

It's true there's nothing new under the sun. Back in 1931 a prospectus was issued for the New Zealand Co-operative Scouring & Carbonising Co Ltd, which later became the New Zealand Co-operative Wool Marketing Association Ltd. As a grower-owned marketing company, it aimed to bypass the auction system, source wools direct from the farmer and market scoured lots of uniform quality. Over the next 50 years the company grew to the stage where it owned and operated five scouring plants, had more than 11,000 members (probably a quarter of commercial sheep farms, together with many small holdings), and at its peak it handled about 8 per cent of the wool clip. Ultimately it failed — the location of its scouring plant was a disadvantage when container shipping was introduced; always seriously under-capitalised, it was unable to build adequate reserves due to pressure from shareholders to rebate profits, and obligations to take wool from supplier shareholders made it a weak seller. Eventually it was absorbed into the Mair wool group in the late 1980s.[1]

So what's different now?

Wool's time has come, big time — there are now significant groups of consumers prepared to make ethical buying decisions around what they eat, what they wear, the car they drive and what they have in their homes. Today manufacturers are prepared to pay $1.50 a kilo more for 'organic' wool — quite a premium when your base price is only $2.50 a kilo.

It is fantastic that Fonterra, our huge dairy company, has done so well for New Zealand, but I strongly believe we need agricultural diversity and a healthy sheep industry alongside it.

Of course, two years ago you wouldn't have found me arguing so emphatically about all this, discussing wool clips and carpet specifications and shearing seasons. I'd have been talking to business groups about unbundling and cellular networks. But now it seems like one of the most important things I could be doing for this country and its future.

Maybe it's the Catholic in me that makes me want to devote my time to things I truly believe in (I once saw a play called *Once a*

Catholic and laughed all the way through because it was so accurate). I've always been attracted to heroic female figures in the church; my early heroines were Joan of Arc and the great mystic saints such as Catherine of Siena and Teresa of Avila. As I've got older it's become more and more important that my heart is in what I am doing. My new passion for wool is clearly based around a commercial company, but for me it's also a mission.

It's a long way from Telecom — but perhaps not so far from Rotorua, where I grew up.

Chapter two

chief
girl

My parents, John and Marion Gattung, arrived in New Zealand in August 1961 as immigrants from Britain. My father was from East London and my mother from Essex. They were part of the wave of immigrants called the ten-pound Poms — in the early 1960s, if you were a married couple in the United Kingdom and one of you secured a job in New Zealand, the New Zealand government paid your passage if you paid £10 and signed a document saying you would stay for at least two years. My father wanted to leave Britain in search of a better life for the family that he intended to have and my mother was up for the adventure. Neither of them was from a family with high aspirations — no one from either of their families had ever been to university and they pretty much stayed living in the vicinity in which they were born. My father had experienced a taste of life in the army in North Africa in Benghazi, Libya, from 1954 to 1956 (as Sapper Gattung of the Royal Engineers), which had whetted his appetite for doing something different with his life. Wherever opportunity for emigration had come up first, New Zealand or Australia, they would have gone, and New Zealand it was.

I was born in Wellington in April 1962, the eldest of four girls. I had a very happy and fairly uneventful childhood, firstly in Wellington and then from the age of eight in Rotorua, where we shifted when Dad got a better job. My father worked in local government — initially as a draftsman and later as a town planner. Entrepreneurial and resourceful, he also invested in commercial property. He encouraged my mother to go into business and in between looking after us she made the most of her sewing talents, setting up a business making tourist souvenirs such as bags and kitchen items.

I was a typical eldest child; apparently I once told my grandparents, Alf and Betty Clay, when they also emigrated from Britain a few years after my parents, that I was the 'chief girl'. Our parents encouraged all of us to strive and told us that it was possible to achieve anything we wanted in life if we worked hard enough and had the determination. My father had five sisters and no brothers, so he has always been very comfortable with women and never recognised any barriers to what we four girls could do compared to boys. My parents were very involved in supporting me and my sisters in all our activities — active in the swimming club we joined and regularly coming to watch me play hockey.

They valued education very highly, so doing well at school was very important in my childhood. I went to St Mary's, a small Roman Catholic primary school, and then McKillop College, a small girls' Roman Catholic secondary school. At that time there were many nuns and so the school provided a living example of female leadership and role models.

It wasn't till I was 17 and took some maths classes with the boys at Edmund Rice College, the Christian Brothers boys' school next door, that I came across any discrimination and encountered the view that there were some things, namely maths, that boys were supposed to be better at than girls. By the time I was 17 I had a pretty well-established world view, so overall this had little impact on my sense of self. And yet it probably did impact on my perspective of how good I was at maths. As women everywhere know, being undermined can be quite insidious.

Still, it was a great time and place to be young and female. When I was born, John F Kennedy had just came to power. The '60s and '70s was a time when the world was steeped in optimism, a time when women believed they could change society by raising its consciousness of women's issues. The exhortation that women could do anything they wanted seemed to be in the very air. An article in *The Listener* in July 2004 put it well: 'There was optimism that change could occur in women's lives — and in men's — through a process of consciousness raising and understanding.'[2] And New Zealand, in 1893 the first country in the world to give the vote to women, prides itself on being a country where there are equal opportunities for all.

My impression of Rotorua in general at that time was of a 'can do' place. Tourism was then, and remains now, one of the main industries and many operations were run by entrepreneurs rather than corporate interests. It was quite a commercial place, with a very strong small-business focus. Since going to university I've never returned to Rotorua for an extended period, but I still have an affinity for the Bay of Plenty and that combination of bush and beach so close at hand which characterised the physical landscape of my childhood.

High school was a happy time for me. I had lots of friends and enjoyed being a member of the school hockey team, although I was by no means a star player, being more enthusiastic than talented.

Two of my personal characteristics stood out in those days. First, I was very curious about lots of things. My best friend Anne Dibley and I (we were later joint dux in seventh form) chose to take an extra subject at senior level so that we could fit in everything we wanted to study in the curriculum. Between fifth, sixth and seventh form I studied almost the entire range of subjects possible, from English and maths through the sciences (biology and chemistry) and languages (French), to geography, history and economics.

Secondly, I was bossy. I can still remember a school prizegiving rehearsal when I presumed to suggest to the principal that there were better ways of organising the event. She asked me to follow her into her office, whereupon she proceeded to suggest that if I continued to be bossy I would never have a happy marriage. I thought she had rocks in her head, though, like most of the nuns at the school, I quite liked her.

Growing up in New Zealand outside the main centres usually means leaving home quite young to pursue opportunities, and this was the case for me. I was 17 when I left Rotorua to make my own way, to do a business degree at Waikato University in Hamilton, but I came back for the summer breaks. I was a swimming pool attendant by day and a waitress at the posh Aorangi Peak restaurant by night.

From quite a young age I was clear that I was going to go to university, although when it came to the crunch I had some difficulty deciding what to study. Deep down I wanted to be a lawyer, but at this time — the early 1980s — there was a surfeit of law graduates. On an open-day visit to Waikato University I was very taken with the management school and both the business and non-business subjects you could study within its four-year programme. And besides, my then boyfriend was going there to study science. He and I split up in the first year, as many school romances do, but I found I really enjoyed studying management and more generally the experience of being at university. I did a Bachelor of Management Studies with a double major in economics and marketing and got honours, managing to include in my four years some Japanese and women's studies papers as part of the politics programme at the university. My sister Angela later became proficient in Japanese and taught it, but I never really did anything with it. I decided I didn't really have a natural ear for languages.

Emotionally, my time at university was dominated by falling in love with David, who later came out as gay. We remain friends to this day, though he's lived in New York for the last 12 years. I remain his one and only girlfriend. He was my first serious boyfriend and it was a short-lived but very intense relationship. For a while after he came out we both thought it might be possible to continue to have a relationship and together we devoured all the books we could find — we both loved reading — about relationships between gay men and straight women. But of course events took their course and he fell in love with a man. I was heartbroken and for some time I struggled to get out of bed in the morning and face the day. My natural positivity deserted me and I wore out my girlfriend and flatmate, Nikki, pouring my heart out to her.

However, in my economics classes I met John Savage, my future long-term partner. He was from Hamilton and was studying economics and politics as part of a social sciences degree. I was drawn to him because he was kind and attentive and I felt very comfortable with him, and we became friends.

I was surrounded by men at business school — there were only a few female students, most of them majoring in accounting, but the lecturers, mainly men, were very encouraging of us. I can remember quite clearly the day I sat in my room reading Helen Place's book about women in management in New Zealand[3] and thinking that it would be really cool to be running a large public company by the time I was 40. I had no idea then that I would be the first woman to do just that; I assumed some other woman would reach that milestone long before I got there.

I wasn't a swot compared to some of the Asian students in terms of the hours I put into study, but I was certainly very focused. I learnt quite early on that each lecturer had a different style and was looking for different things, and tried to quickly figure out what was required in each situation. I worked reasonably hard but not obsessively, enjoying playing badminton, and spent lots of time with my friends — although I never got into drinking alcohol and to this day drink very little.

Although I enjoyed management school, I never really felt like I fitted in. I was always too flamboyant and too opinionated. I even wore suits to lectures, as did David. Not surprisingly, we stood out! I remember one day some of the students in a business school class were passing pornographic magazines along the rows of seats and I stood up and voiced my objection to it. On the other hand, I didn't fit in any better with the entirely female groups in my women's studies classes. There, I felt like I had the word 'capitalist' emblazoned on my forehead because I was the only person taking women's studies papers as part of a management studies degree rather than as part of an arts or social sciences degree.

At the end of our third year at business school, every student had to complete a three-month project over the summer holidays. I was accepted by Fisher & Paykel and did a market-research project on refrigerators. They offered me a job at the end of my degree and I thought long and hard about accepting it because I was attracted to the culture of the company, but I still had a hankering to do law.

So at the end of business school, aged 21, I headed off to Wellington and enrolled in law school at Victoria University. John Savage and I were now a couple, and he had accepted a job as an economist in the Department of Labour. John and I had first started living together as a couple in our last year at university in Hamilton (having transitioned from being flatmates during the course of the year, as you do!), which had made his mother a bit upset, but by the time we moved to Wellington it didn't seem to be an issue for either set of parents, even though both were Catholics.

As I didn't want to spend several more years with no income, the summer before I started my second degree I rang Television New Zealand to see if there were any jobs I could get with my business degree, specifically the marketing aspect. Fortuitously, I found out the market research officer was leaving, so there was a position available at TVNZ's sales and marketing office, at that time in Wellington. It was my plan to study full time and work part time, though it didn't work out like that and after a while I found myself both enrolled as a full-time student *and* working full time at TVNZ!

I never really enjoyed law school, although I did make one or two lifelong friends there. I realised quite early on that being a lawyer was not me. I didn't like the 'hired gun' nature of it, the arguing one side and then the other, just for the sake of it. I prefer to be part of the action rather than an eloquent spectator talking about it afterwards. Nevertheless, I decided to persevere with the degree because I thought it would be useful in a business career.

On the other hand, I enjoyed my work at TVNZ immensely. I loved the interface with clients and 15 months into the job I was promoted, so that I had a team of staff reporting to me, publishing a weekly magazine for advertising agency clients. I felt in my element taking responsibility and really enjoyed leading a team. I was extremely busy, working on a range of publications, leading the team in their activities and every day racing up The Terrace to attend lectures, then doing the required coursework in the evenings.

Nevertheless, after a few years at TVNZ I felt I wanted to do something which combined my law and business degrees. I decided to get into merchant banking, which was big at the time, in the pre-crash mid '80s. I tried very hard to break into the industry, but got the clear message that women did not fit in — of course, the 'thanks, but no thanks' letters didn't say that, but one man who interviewed me told me that later, over the phone. I was flabbergasted.

My father had always instilled in me that when one door closed in your face, you had to try to find a window. So in 1987 I sucessfully applied for the job of marketing research manager at National Mutual (known as AXA since 2000, after the large French company bought 51 per cent of the company in 1995). To all intents and purposes it looked like a sideways move; TVNZ was a more glamorous, high-profile company and I had responsibility for staff in my role there, whereas at National Mutual I was going back to being a sole operator. While I'd given up on the idea of merchant banking at this point, I was still keen to get a foothold in the financial services industry because I saw it as a logical place to combine my business and law qualifications, so I was prepared to make a shift into the unknown. However, soon after taking that job I was promoted to the role of acting marketing manager (when my boss who'd been the marketing manager was asked to take on a special assignment), with a bigger team than I'd ever had before. I loved it, and a few months later I was officially appointed to the marketing manager role.

I began to feel like I was really on the way.

first rungs on the ladder

Unfortunately, my first year at National Mutual was marred by the longest period of physical pain I've endured in my life. I experienced a whole year of indescribable, abscess-like pain in my teeth, an ache that never went away. I begged my dentist to drill my teeth as I assumed it must be an abscess deep in the root.

I can remember the day John and I bought our first house: a small cottage up numerous steps on a steep Wellington hillside. I remember the multiple trips up the path and steps, carrying our belongings. By the end of the day I was just exhausted with pain.

Over a period of time, I had several of my teeth root-filled, but nothing took the pain away. Finally my dentist said she didn't know what was causing the pain, but it definitely wasn't my teeth. She said she wasn't drilling any more of them and referred me to the head of dentistry at Wellington Hospital. He concluded that I was suffering from temporomandibular joint syndrome — TMJ for short — an inflammation of the joint between the jaw and the skull which he said was largely brought about by stress. Who, me? Stressed? Of course not. Must be talking about somebody else! He gave me a bite plate to wear while I was asleep which more or less held the symptoms at bay, but didn't deal with any underlying cause. I also went to an alternative health practitioner, who put me on a rigorous diet and sent me to an osteopath. I got a lot of relief from regularly seeing the osteopath and learnt to manage stress better — exercising by swimming every day, cutting out caffeine and getting regular massages. Over time the symptoms subsided and then disappeared completely.

Pain aside, my years at National Mutual were very interesting for me because much of my working time was spent with the agency sales force. These people, nearly all men, were not employees — essentially they were independent businesspeople who earned a commission selling financial and insurance products, and who had chosen to represent National Mutual and sell its products. They were mobile, opinionated and their own bosses. The dynamic was very interactive, very direct. I had no positional power over them, so I learnt first-hand about the importance of 'personal power' — the power of passion, persuasion and being myself in a business situation.

I really enjoyed my time there but eventually got tired of being paraded as the 'token woman' in middle management. I was the only woman chosen to go on a senior management potential programme with other middle managers from New Zealand, Australia and Hong Kong. I realised that due to the inherent conservatism of the industry it was going to be very hard to advance further, so I decided that when the right opportunity arose I would leave.

Soon after completing that programme, I saw an advertisement for the role of chief manager – marketing at the Bank of New Zealand. I called up the recruiter on a Friday afternoon, who told me it was too late because he was presenting the shortlist to the Bank of New Zealand's chief executive, Lindsay Pyne, the following Monday. When I said, 'We've got the weekend', he replied, 'Well, only if you can drive to Taupo and meet me at my bach' — so I did. Clearly I made the right impression, as I made it onto the shortlist and was interviewed the following week on behalf of Lindsay by Rod Carr, who was chief manager – financial services, and then by Lindsay himself. Almost before I knew it I was the new chief manager – marketing at the Bank of New Zealand. I was very chuffed. I could hardly believe how smoothly this process had happened and I was very much looking forward to working there. I was so conscientious, though, that I worked well into the evening on my last day at National Mutual tidying things up and had to be dragged off to my farewell party.

The day I joined the BNZ in September 1990, Lindsay Pyne asked me to come up to his office. He told me that the bank had serious balance sheet issues and needed a financial injection from the government to the tune of several hundred million dollars. He hadn't been able to tell me this during the interview process of course, because it was very closely held information. Suddenly I discovered that instead of joining an organisation I thought was on the up and up, it was facing a big down. The 'bail out' of the BNZ was huge news. The ethos of the management team was totally about working together to restore the position of the bank.

My years at the BNZ with Lindsay as CEO were among the most terrific learning curve of my business career. The executive team he pulled together was second to none. It included Rob Fyfe, now CEO of Air New Zealand; Rod Carr, who's had a distinguished public and private sector career and is now vice-chancellor of Canterbury University; Sam Knowles, now CEO of Kiwibank; Tom Gallagher, who became CEO of Westpac in New Zealand; and Peter Thodey, who became CEO of the BNZ. Two of Lindsay's passions were building the brand and developing people capability in the company, and my time at the bank was marked by working hard in both these areas and learning a lot.

One advertising campaign that I led over this time stands out in particular. The aim was to bridge the BNZ's strong corporate identity with specific banking products, while retaining its warm, familiar tone of New Zealandness. The series of commercials produced by Colenso that ran through 1992 and 1993 — Business Talk, Farming Talk, Mortgage Talk, Retirement Talk and Investment Talk — were highly original and featured offbeat humour. Three commercials from the Talk campaign took out top honours at the CLIO advertising awards in New York, with one beating 7100 entries from 50 countries to win the inaugural Best of Show award. Commercials from this campaign also won awards at the London International Awards and the Australasian Television Awards. Most of the major industry papers raved about them and this quote from the *New York Post* was typical: 'A small agency in New Zealand beat out the most powerful shops in the world last night to take Madison Ave's most coveted prize. For the first time in CLIO's 34-year history the judges awarded a Best of Show category. It took two ballots, unanimous each time, to pick Colenso as the winner'.[4]

But it was not only people in the advertising fraternity who thought the work was outstanding. Viewers took a shine to the human qualities portrayed by the quirky, distinctively New Zealand humour, and the advertising campaigns and the bank's focus on working with staff to give excellent customer service paid huge dividends in terms of stabilising the bank's customer base and restoring its image.

One of the biggest and most interesting projects that I worked on while at the BNZ was the 1992 America's Cup challenge in San Diego. The bank was one of the key sponsors of the New Zealand Challenge and we created a supporters' club that the whole country got behind. Another project I really enjoyed setting up was the BNZ-sponsored Kiwi Recovery programme, which is still going to this day.

Marketing of this type was a huge part of the first 15 years of my career. While I am very comfortable with numbers — I can look at a balance sheet or a profit and loss statement and know what to focus on, seeing patterns and immediately identifying any irregularities in the numbers — I've never really been fascinated by them. At university I saw accounting papers as simply courses I had to take to get my management degree.

From the time I was a teenager, helping my mother sell the souvenirs she made, I have been very interested in the whole product sales/marketing aspect of business. By nature I am both analytical and creative, and I think marketing is a creative outlet in many ways.

My first full-time job, at TVNZ, gave me a very good grounding in the ways of media and advertising agencies as part of a marketing game plan. A strong relationship with an advertising agency is one of the most exhilarating and reinforcing assets a marketing person can have. The best advertising people have a passion for the brand and bring a different perspective to it than those from inside the company. If you have a high turnover of marketing staff, as can be the case, then often it is people at the agency who have a continuity of understanding about the heritage of the brand, which aspects need to be retained and celebrated, and what needs to be refreshed.

I always regarded the advertising agency people I worked with as external members of the marketing team. I never played games like putting them up to pitch to re-win business because I think people have to feel valued as key members of a team to give their best, rather than always being on edge. Advertising agencies often feel very unsettled when the head of marketing and/or the CEO of one of their major clients changes. The nature of agency–client relationships means they often go wrong from the ground up at times of change. The account director, creative director and CEO of the ad agency might have great relationships with the marketing director or CEO of the company, but product managers in the marketing team further down the pecking order don't necessarily feel that they are being listened to or supported, or given the priority they believe they and their products deserve. Over time this can be corrosive and can sometimes erupt or otherwise come to the fore when there is a change of guard at the top.

My three favourite marketing campaigns of my career so far were the 1992 America's Cup campaign for the BNZ, the 1995 Telecom 'talk as long as you like for $5' campaign and the 2004 Telecom launch of 3G mobile in New Zealand. All were marked by a bold idea, fresh in both vision and execution, with a total partnership between the client and the agency and a small, talented, enthusiastic team working on execution.

I was in my element working at the BNZ, enjoying being a leader and working on creative campaigns. Unfortunately, it wasn't to last. In 1992 National Australia Bank bought the BNZ and the Australians came across to run the bank, as Lindsay Pyne left to take up a senior position with Visa in Asia.

My world changed overnight. NAB is a very successful Australian bank with its own way of doing things and even though by its own standards it probably gave the BNZ huge autonomy, it felt like a much more constrained environment to me. I now had to ask permission and get sign-off from people who knew nothing about the New Zealand market, instead of being able to directly authorise major campaigns and initiatives after consultation with Lindsay. And once again, as a woman I felt I would not be able to advance any further. I was upset about the changes to my working environment and felt so blocked again, agonising over what to do for several months.

Then one day I'd just had enough. I'd had to do one too many presentations to visiting Australians. I started to think about life after BNZ and what I wanted to achieve next. My dream of running a big New Zealand company by the age of 40 still burned in me and maybe this crisis was another opportunity.

Chapter four

a lucky meeting

One day while driving home in mid-1994, I had a wee altercation with one of Wellington's famous hills: I turned uphill into the wrong street then found I couldn't reverse straight back down. I flagged down a passing motorist to help me with my stranded car. My saviour turned out to be Tom Potrykus, then general manager – marketing at Telecom, an American who'd been with the company for a few years and was soon to go home. After chatting with him, I decided to go for his job. Being head of marketing at Telecom was an exciting prospect, as it was one of the few marketing jobs in New Zealand bigger than the one I had at the BNZ.

I tried without success through various contacts to get my name on the shortlist for the job, then I read in the business media that the company had concluded that there were no New Zealanders suitable for the role, so they were looking offshore. I decided I needed to take matters into my own hands, so I called up Telecom and asked to be put through to the office of the CEO, Roderick Deane. I had never met Roderick, and of course I wasn't put through to him, but the woman who answered the phone had the presence of mind to pass my details on to the general manager of human resources, David Bedford. David called, and I went over to Telecom and met with him straight away.

David was an experienced, astute executive and a very measured person and he didn't give much away at our meeting, so I was delighted when he called me at home that night and asked me to come and meet Roderick first thing the next morning. I was very nervous walking into Roderick's office. Previously the chairman of the State Services Commission, deputy governor of the Reserve Bank and chief executive of the Electricity Corporation, Roderick's reputation was formidable. It was hard not to be thrown when I first met Roderick because his intellect was obvious from the minute we started talking, and of course he knew lots about telecommunications and I knew nothing. He also knew a huge amount about banking, of course. About 15 minutes into our conversation he asked if I would like a cup of tea, which I took as a good sign and started to relax a little! Anyway, after interviews with David, Roderick, Ben McMillan (then Telecom's chief operating officer) and the recruitment agency, and the normal amount of reference checking, I was offered the job of general manager – marketing in August 1994. I would report to McMillan, a very experienced American telecommunications operating executive. I was overjoyed and couldn't wait to start.

I enjoyed my 18 months in this role immensely. Towards the end of my time at the BNZ I had started to feel quite stuck in a box, and at Telecom I felt freed up again. I had a large marketing budget, a lot of people in the marketing team and plenty of opportunity to make a difference.

These 18 months were a tumultuous period in terms of tele-communications pricing, as we drastically reduced international and national calling prices. I can clearly remember where I was when Bruce Parkes, my head of strategy, suggested the idea of customers paying no more than $5 to talk as long as they liked, to anyone, any-where in New Zealand. I thought it was a brilliant idea and we drove the initiative through. People told us it changed their lives — getting in touch with old friends and relatives and rekindling relationships. Similar strategies were later adopted by telecommunications com-panies elsewhere in the world and it revolutionised the way people thought about calling long distance within New Zealand, which previously had nearly always been charged by the minute and was perceived as expensive.

After 18 months Ben McMillan retired and returned to the United States, and in early 1996 I became group general manager – services, reporting directly to Roderick. This was my big break. I was now responsible for revenues of over $3 billion, all sales as well as marketing and many of the company's core services such as call centres and retail outlets, though not the network side of the business, which was managed by Ken Benson.

It was during this time that the focus of the business started to move away from calling towards data services. The internet began to go mainstream and we launched Xtra, Telecom's internet service provider. We made the decision to invest in the Southern Cross cable — an undersea fibre cable linking Australia and New Zealand with North America — in order to access increased data capacity which we expected would be required over the next decade, and announced outsourcing deals to US company EDS for IT and French company Alcatel on the network side. Telecommunications is an economy-of-scale business and New Zealand isn't big enough to have sufficient scale. We wanted to simulate scale by standardising and working with global partners.

I put a lot of time and focus into understanding the various parts of the business. I had previously had around 200 staff in marketing and I now had 3500! I spent time with a wide range of people, both at the coalface and in 'skip level' meetings, i.e. meetings with the people who reported to the people who directly reported to me. It's very easy to get stuck in middle management, especially if you are a woman. I'd always been very focused on going further. I'd always tried to hire people smarter than me and build a good team so that I could be promoted. And I'd always sought to work in areas that really mattered to the company's fortunes, which increases your visibility. I placed a premium on having a very strong team around me, created by a combination of promoting people already in the company who I felt were capable of bigger roles and bringing people in from the outside. One of the people I promoted several times during my period at Telecom was Mark Ratcliffe, a very capable all-round executive who I particularly valued, not just for his deep understanding of telecommunications and IT in general and Telecom processes in particular, but also for his common sense. He later became my chief information officer when I was chief executive. One of the people I brought in from outside was Peter Thompson, another experienced IT executive, who looked after our corporate business.

It was in this role that for the first time I experienced colleagues who were continually trying to put me off my stride: one a man, and one a woman. It was generally covert, but I learnt to expect a shot across my bows a couple of days before any important executive committee meeting. I was hurt by this and found it very unsettling, as it was intended to be. I think they both felt threatened by me, reasonably recently arrived on the scene and now having a plum role, and one of them at least had ambitions of becoming CEO. I experienced first-hand that women do not always support each other at the top of the corporate pyramid and I vowed that I would not be like that. I had a very loyal team, one or two of whom did point duty watching my back for me. I made sure I communicated directly with Roderick often and I cultivated my own sources who were close to him, so they could help represent my perspective.

During this period a good chunk of the company was still owned by the original cornerstone shareholders, American telecommunications companies Ameritech and Bell Atlantic. Telecom was established in 1987 as a state-owned enterprise to take over the telecommunications network services previously operated by the Post Office, and from

April 1, 1989 all telecommunications markets in New Zealand had been open to competition. The process of fully privatising Telecom was completed in September 1990 by its sale for $4.25 billion to a consortium including Bell Atlantic and Ameritech, and these companies still had representatives on the board.

I attended several board meetings in America and found them rather formal affairs, marked by graciousness and good etiquette, but there was no mistaking the underlying message: the only thing that mattered was the bottom line. Executives in these companies, and by extension companies which they wholly or partially owned, either made their budget numbers or were swiftly exited. There were absolutely no points for trying or being nice.

I am not saying that such a single-minded focus on the short-term bottom line is necessarily a good strategy for business success — I don't think it is — but that's how it was, and if you took a role as a senior executive in those companies, those were the rules you had to play by. In deeply conservative, old-school corporate America, women seldom broke through to senior roles in these companies, and I desperately wanted to make it to the very top.

It was part-way through one rather grim board meeting in Chicago that Roderick passed me a note around the table. I thought it would be a message about something he wanted me to say — or, more likely, something he *didn't* want me to say — but instead it was an advertisement he had torn out of a magazine about a clothes shop in California he thought I might like to visit on my way home! During this period he was generally very supportive of me and I chuckled to myself that he had correctly 'read' that one of the ways I was getting through the board meeting was thinking about what nice things I'd do next. Although I worked hard I hadn't forgotten my lesson from many years earlier about managing my workload and always made sure I had time for friends and activities outside work.

Also, around the age of 30 I'd taken up horse riding and found I really enjoyed it. In October 1998 a horse I'd had for only a few months, Spy, bolted while I was riding him. It all happened in a split second, but as he took off I knew there was no way I could stay on. I put my right arm out to break my fall in order to protect my head and back, but as soon as I hit the ground I knew that I had badly smashed my right wrist. I was taken to hospital by ambulance and doped up with painkillers while the doctors decided what to do. They thought there was a reasonable chance they could fix my wrist by putting it in a cast and that I wouldn't need an operation to have it pinned, but the first time they tried it didn't set correctly, so they had to do it again. The second time the procedure was successful and I was sent home with a cast, but it was the old-fashioned style which meant I couldn't get it wet.

It's surprising how debilitating having a broken wrist is. Roderick was very kind and arranged for a car to pick me up each morning to bring me in to work because I couldn't drive. I couldn't dress myself, I couldn't wash my hair, I couldn't write and the painkillers made me feel a bit disoriented. But for me the worst thing was not being able to swim.

After eight weeks the cast was removed and though my wrist was very weak, it was bliss to get back in the water and do very gentle breaststroke. The doctors warned me that I might not get full mobility back in my wrist, but I credit a wonderful Chinese healer who I saw in Wellington with helping me restore the tendons after the bone had mended.

I never rode Spy again because I no longer trusted him, but a few months later I started riding a less spirited horse, Pride, who I have been riding ever since, more or less without incident. While the saying goes 'Pride comes before a fall', in my case Pride came after the fall!

great expectations

From the day I joined Telecom I had seen the possibility that I might be able to become CEO. In Roderick Deane I recognised someone who valued intelligence and a person's ability to get things done highly, perhaps above all else. And those have always been two of my hallmarks. I also realised, being one of three women on his executive team and observing his desire to find a woman to join the Telecom board, that he was someone who valued diversity and was not sexist, unlike the cultures of my two previous employers.

Like everybody else at Telecom, I had no idea that in February 1999 Roderick was going to announce that he would succeed Peter Shirtcliffe as chairman of Telecom in October that year, and that a search would begin for his successor as CEO. I had been at Telecom for nearly five years by then, and from the moment this move was announced I went into 'Project CEO' mode.

The other internal candidate was an American, Jeff White,

who had been Telecom's chief financial officer for several years and was very highly regarded. Jeff and I had always got on well and continued to work together effectively during this period. It was rather a long time for the company to be in a leadership transition, with the board running an exhaustive search process, interviewing both myself and Jeff as well as other New Zealand candidates and searching both the UK and North American markets.

A global recruiting firm was appointed to undertake the search, and I met with the US-based recruiter in New York while on a business trip to talk to investors. Telecom had and still has a high proportion of US fund managers on its share register. When Bell Atlantic and Ameritech paid some $4.25 billion for the business in 1990, an unheard-of sum at the time, there was great interest in America about the company and from the early 1990s it had a high proportion of North American investors, which necessitated regular trips there.

The interviews with the board, however, took place in New Zealand. I got a whole new wardrobe from Adrienne Winkelmann — black skirt and trouser suits and silk shirts — for the interview process, and practised my interview skills with eight discreet, intelligent people from outside Telecom role-playing each of the directors who'd be interviewing me. I had them ask me the sort of questions I thought the directors would ask (and indeed, in the real interview I did get asked one or two questions that were exactly as I had practised and practised in the role plays). I felt quite excited during the process as I had nothing to lose — few commentators picked that I would get the role, and many thought it would go to someone outside Telecom. I felt slightly nervous being interviewed by the whole board, but quite comfortable during the one-on-one interviews with individual board members as I had presented to them and worked with them for several years.

On Thursday, August 12, 1999 it was announced that I would become the chief executive officer of Telecom New Zealand on October 1 — the first woman to head such a major, multibillion-dollar company in this country. I was so excited, I rushed home to discuss the draft contract with John and nearly sideswiped several cars on the way. I am not a good driver at the best of times and that day I was a long way from being in a calm and steady state! This was my dream come true, the moment I had worked towards for nearly 20 years since I had sat in my room in Hamilton, reading Helen Place's book and setting my goal. I had been brought up to believe that anything was possible and now, at the age of 37, with a couple of years to spare, I had proved it.

My joy that day and the next was indescribable as friends and colleagues contacted me and rushed to my office. In the five years I'd been at Telecom I'd formed very close bonds with many of the people who worked with and for me, and many of them were extroverts who weren't slow to communicate their pleasure, first of all that it was an internal appointment and secondly that it was me. I got a fax from someone who was with the consumer marketing team when the announcement came through, who told me they'd jumped out of their seats and cheered when they heard that I had got the job.

The response that first day and for the next couple of weeks was completely overwhelming. I received literally hundreds of letters, emails, faxes and calls from people I'd worked with over the previous 20 years, but also many from complete strangers. The common theme was that my appointment was seen as inspirational because I was a woman, reasonably young and a New Zealander, and because I had achieved my dream. I received many, many letters from women who said they felt if it could happen for me then they, too, would be able to achieve their dreams. This came not long after Hewlett Packard in the United States had named Carly Fiorina as its new CEO. Women know that women have a more difficult job climbing the corporate ladder than men, so there was a lot of collective tapping together of heels when it happened for me.

The media coverage of my appointment was extensive — wall to wall — and the pictures showed how delighted I was. While many in the telecommunications community had speculated privately that I could be a contender for the job, it was only a few months earlier, in

May 1999, that a small profile of me had been part of a story called 'Ten Powerful People You've Never Heard Of'[5]. In the wider world it was an absolutely unheralded move, and the surprise of it made it very newsworthy.

I felt a funny mixture of exhilaration and nerves during the media conference to announce my appointment. I was totally unprepared for the flash bulbs going off in my face and the microphones being thrust at me. And as Adrienne Perry, a journalist who was there later commented, some of the questions I was asked were utterly astonishing.[6] I was asked about my marital status and if I intended to have children. Adrienne said that the men in the room seemed gobsmacked by the appointment, and the novelty value of having a woman at the top of corporate New Zealand was huge. And of course it complemented the wider story about leadership roles for women in New Zealand, with Jenny Shipley as Prime Minister and Helen Clark as Leader of the Opposition, Dame Margaret Bazley having run the largest government department and Sian Elias being recently named Chief Justice. Interestingly, Jenny Shipley sent me flowers and a note of great warmth but Helen Clark did not contact me.

Adrienne wrote that I was very direct and could be off-putting, but if I had been a quiet, polite and measured woman, I would not have got to the top. And there in a nutshell lies the dilemma for women in leadership roles. Nobody follows a person who doesn't have confidence in themselves and a clear sense of where they're headed. And yet, if a woman is too strong, she can come across as aggressive and off-putting. Adrienne also predicted that the obsession with my gender was likely to remain.

My appointment also came as a profound surprise to the financial community, who had been backing Jeff White to get the job. At best they were neutral about my appointment, although I realised quite quickly that actually most were negative. However, Telecom's share price hardly moved on the announcement, so clearly my appointment didn't faze the market too much.

The six weeks between the announcement and my actually

becoming CEO were filled with interviews and messages of wonderment, surprise and congratulations. It was truly a halcyon period: getting all the glory for getting the job, but not yet actually doing it. Once you are CEO, as a fellow CEO and friend remarked to me, you never want for company, and this was certainly the case during this period. All sorts of people came out of the woodwork claiming to be my long-lost best friend. I tend to trust people until it's been demonstrated that I shouldn't, and there's no doubt that during this period I was inundated with a mixture of people who were very genuine and those who were simply positioning themselves in the best possible light, often would-be product or service suppliers. Even though it was possible to discern between the two groups, I am only human and I remember one day realising how easy it would be to have all the attention go to my head.

I'm very plain speaking, I'm very straight talking — perhaps to the point of rather too much bluntness — and I made a decision there and then that I would continue to surround myself with people who told it to me like it was, which had always been my own style. After swimming one morning, which I do every day as a combination of exercise and meditation, I resolved to always try to be true to my spirit and not be captured by ego. It's impossible to get to the top without a strong ego and I believe that to achieve you need to have a strong sense of self, but I wanted to stay grounded and real.

Over the next eight years, there was a week-in, week-out constant barrage of reports on Telecom and on me, some of it positive, some of it negative, some of it neutral. All through those years I assumed that because Telecom was New Zealand's largest company by market capitalisation on the stock market, it and whoever was its CEO would receive that much coverage. But in the two years since I left, the profile of my male successor, Paul Reynolds, has been so much more muted, I've come to the view that Adrienne Perry was right — that the intense scrutiny I faced from the minute my appointment was announced was at least partly to do with my gender.

becoming the boss

I can remember my first day as CEO very clearly. David Knight, who was a senior lawyer at Telecom, brought me a paper on issues to do with interconnection with Clear that he needed a decision on. I remember reading it and thinking gosh, suddenly people expect me to have all the answers. I had run Telecom's retail businesses for several years, but there was a very strong Chinese wall between the retail business and the teams which dealt with interconnection with our competitors. There was a very strong protocol that information about telecommunications companies interconnecting with Telecom that were competing at the retail level with Telecom was not shared between the interconnection teams and the retail teams, so I simply hadn't been privy to any conversations in that area.

There were one or two people I could ask for advice on the matter, including of course the legal team, but ultimately the buck stopped with me. It was a small example of what I found almost immediately:

it's one thing to be on the executive team reporting to the CEO, which I had been for over five years at Telecom and four years previously at the BNZ, but it's quite another thing to be in the hot seat yourself.

My first and most immediate challenge was choosing my team. Jeff White told me almost immediately that he was going to head back to the United States. He had originally come to Telecom on a three- or four-year assignment and had stayed seven years. He had always intended to return and not getting the CEO role sped up that process. There were absolutely no hard feelings between us — we'd always worked well together as colleagues and during 1999, when we had both been in the running for the CEO role, I think we'd done a really good job of continuing to work together constructively.

Jeff's imminent departure left a huge gap in my management team, however, particularly as I didn't have a financial background. I needed to find a first-rate chief financial officer quickly. The other huge gap was my old job, running the retail businesses. Rob Fyfe had been working for me as general manager – consumer for about a year and the succession strategy had always been that he would replace me as group general manager for the New Zealand business if I became CEO. However, about the time that my appointment as CEO was announced, he was offered a role as CEO with a media company in the UK, which he accepted. It was a great opportunity for him, but it meant that I now had the two most important roles to fill.

I had a lot of respect for the group of people who had been my colleagues on Roderick's executive team, and with only one exception wanted them to continue pretty much in their existing roles. So I was hurt when I realised quite early on that they were profoundly unsettled by my promotion and were either only grudgingly supportive of me or totally unsupportive. But I was too focused and busy to let it slow me down. And the unexpected resignation of another of my old colleagues, who I had really wanted to retain on the team, did provide the opportunity to bring in someone equally good from outside the company.

Then of course there were other people who saw my appointment as an opportunity and genuinely wanted to be part of the new regime. For example, Bruce Parkes jumped at the chance to establish and take on a new role of general manager – government relations. Bruce and I had been a great team from my first day in Telecom, when I was general manager – marketing and he was my head of marketing strategy. I thought that Bruce's ability to think laterally, his calm, measured personal demeanour and his previous experience in another regulated sector (electricity) combined to make him a great fit for that role.

One of Roderick's most important legacies was that Telecom's senior management group had become the home of some of the country's best minds. I didn't want to lose that. I wanted to keep the focus on it being a place where intellectual standards were high, but I was equally determined to break down the culture that had built up over many years of almost tribal affiliation to particular areas of the company. This arose in part from a prior organisational model of several separate regional operating companies, combined into one company in 1993, and ongoing separation between the network division and the sales and service division, which saw deep tensions arise regularly.

I set out to build an executive team who were all very smart and competent in their own fields, but who would work well together and put the good of the company ahead of their own particular area. My goal was that they would then role model this to the rest of the organisation. If people looked up and saw an executive team with lots of infighting and backstabbing, there was no way I could build a collegial culture in the rest of the company.

I don't think that focusing strongly on teamwork, as I did throughout my time as CEO at Telecom, is necessarily the model for all organisations. I think it is possible to run a global multinational in different countries, in different industry sectors, without that. But, as a network business with technology overlaps all over the show, operating in a constantly changing dynamic sector, I think a series of fiefdoms would have been a very poor organisational model for Telecom.

The huge news of my appointment meant many invitations to speak to various groups and organisations. Up till that point I hadn't had a particularly high public profile, but now invitations flowed in from all around New Zealand and Australia. I was also invited to join the New Zealand Business Roundtable, which I politely declined. I have never been a particularly ideological person. I have never joined any political party or actively worked on behalf of one. And by nature I tend to distrust people who have a strong ideological agenda. I'm a broad-church sort of person, essentially pragmatic by nature. I distrust institutions where the people at the top tell everyone else what to do, and politicians who have that bent. I believe very strongly in a collegial style. When a person believes that their principles are so self-evident that the rest of us should be required to follow them as well, I naturally rebel. I strongly believe in everybody's right to live a self-determined life, as I have always striven to live mine. And that's one of the reasons why I have never entered politics, although it has been suggested to me on numerous occasions.

Now that I was in the hot seat, I wanted to do my best to get out and promote the company and talk about my vision and plans for it. Also, the investor relations team prevailed on me to go offshore to meet with major fund managers as soon as possible, which I did within a few months of becoming CEO. Actually, in my first week in the role I flew to the United States with the board for meetings with Microsoft and Bill Gates and EDS to cement the links between our companies, as they were now major technology partners.

The financial results for the three months before I became CEO, which I presented to the market for the first time as CEO in November 1999, were pretty uninspiring. Telecom was holding its own in the New Zealand market but not achieving much growth. I was pretty uninspiring delivering them, too. Suddenly, in my first public outing actually doing the job of a CEO, rather than just talking about being the CEO, I got stage fright and presented in a very under-confident manner. The combination of the huge amount of travelling and taking on the CEO job while still doing parts of my old role meant that

I drove myself nearly to the point of exhaustion in those first few months. I hadn't yet got into a rhythm and learnt to pace myself in the way which would later become second nature to me. And things were about to become worse before they got better.

Overall, 1999 had seen a huge run-up in share prices arising from the pre-2000 tech bubble. This carried on into the first few months of 2000, with the Telecom share price rising from around $7.60 the week I started as CEO and reaching all-time high levels above $9.80 in April 2000. And then, in company with its global peers, its share price started to crash and burn. Within weeks of this happening stories were appearing about analysts being unsure whether I was the right person to lead Telecom.

In fact, it was really nothing to do with the share price: they'd been unsure from the beginning, but in the pre-Christmas period the novelty value of the story had drowned out the negativity with which most of the mainly male financial community regarded my appointment. As *The Independent* quietly reported, 'The financial market's view on her is more negative than neutral, said one fund manager, adding that he would have preferred an aggressive American in the job.'[7]

Another important factor placing pressure on the share price was the election in November 1999 of a Labour–Alliance government. As it turned out, in that first term the government was careful not to scare the horses, so to speak, but at the time the change of government cast a pall over all leading New Zealand stocks. I can remember overseas fund managers telling me that they were overweight New Zealand (i.e. they had a larger proportion of New Zealand companies in their share portfolio than New Zealand's size merited), but they would now be reducing their exposure essentially because of the increased risk that a left-leaning government would bring in policies unfavourable to business.

In Telecom's case this was heightened by the specific industry risk. While in opposition, Labour had campaigned on the need for an inquiry into telecommunications, and shortly after it took power

announced that Hugh Fletcher would head such an inquiry into the
sector. This was not really a surprise, but the government's agenda
was made clearer in an official Beehive media release on February
23, 2000, in which acting minister of communications Trevor Mallard
said, 'Many New Zealanders are concerned about Telecom's position
in the market.'

The days of waiting six weeks to get a phone put on had long
been forgotten by the public, and there has always been a degree
of concern among Kiwis about infrastructure perceived as essential
being in private hands. Indeed, in April 2000 a *National Business
Review*–Compaq poll found that 61 per cent of people thought the sale
of Telecom had been a mistake.

Also putting pressure on our share price was Telecom's need to
cut its dividend following its purchase of AAPT, one of Australia's
largest telecommunications carriers. Telecom had bought into AAPT
in mid-1999, at a time when telco valuations were much higher. At the
time Roderick was seen to have got a good price: the media applauded
Telecom for managing to 'steal' AAPT at around AU$5 per share,
when it had been trading for around AU$9. There were cartoons
in Australian newspapers picturing Roderick as a canny miser who
had snapped up AAPT at a bargain basement price. Within a year,
however, the environment had changed and all telco stocks had been
re-rated downwards. Of course, the minute I got the CEO's job it was
my problem. Revaluations like that, of a sector, or a country, or indeed
a global economy as has happened more recently, clearly happen from
time to time. They're almost impossible to predict, although after the
fact, of course, there are always many commentators who will say it
should have been foreseeable.

Unless you've been at the most senior levels of a publicly listed
company and have regularly interfaced with fund managers, it is
hard to describe the sheer lack of sentimentality with which they
approach your company. The financial results of the last quarter or
last year count for less than their view of the company's likely future
performance. Fund managers differ in their investment horizons and

some look longer term than others, but ultimately they're all being judged on the performance of their portfolio, so they apply huge pressure on the CEO and CFO of a company whose stock they hold — occasionally publicly, at times of crisis, but usually behind closed doors. You literally can go from hero to zero — or the other way — on the basis of one quarter's results, or a share-price fluctuation that might have little to do with factors that are in your control. There are organisations which poll the financial community regularly, asking them to rate the performance of CEOs and management teams, the results of which are then presented to the boards of those companies.

For most of the time I was Telecom CEO, part of my bonus depended on doing well in those surveys. I felt I was on the back foot with the analyst community from quite early on because of pressure on the share price due to fallout from the tech bubble bursting.

Over time this got better, partly because I became more of a known entity to some of the leading fund managers, but also because I recruited a first-class chief financial officer, Marko Bogoievski. Marko is a Kiwi Harvard MBA graduate who had previously worked in New Zealand but was at the time in the United States in an entrepreneurial start-up situation. He joined as Telecom CFO in May 2000, just as the share price was starting to tank. Philip King, our very experienced head of investor relations, Marko and I spent a lot of 2000 trying to reassure the market.

I also started the year with an agenda for the company. First, I surrounded myself with the best people I could, particularly those who had skill sets different from mine. I wanted to take Roderick's legacy of Telecom being a place where the best minds gathered and adapt that to one where the best minds respectfully and collegially interacted with everyone else in the organisation, whatever division they were in. Engineers and marketers come from very different perspectives and have a very different take on what's important. Interestingly, when I came to leave Telecom, many people commented that the most significant feature of my time as CEO was the culture shift that I embarked on almost immediately in terms of behaviours I demonstrated and encouraged others to demonstrate.

I strongly believe that, when all is said and done, people often don't remember very clearly the details of what you said to them, or the details of what happened when. But everybody has a lasting impression of how another person made them feel. I tried in all my dealings throughout my time as CEO to make people feel appreciated. With my close colleagues in particular I went to a lot of time and trouble to show in small ways that I saw myself as part of a greater whole. This might be a particularly female perspective. I'm not sure, but it's certainly a key aspect of my personality and leadership style.

So I was very clear on the 'how' agenda — how I wanted to make things happen. I also hit the year running with a very clear 'what' agenda. First, if at all possible, I wanted to create a less litigious relationship with our key competitors — Clear and Telstra. Being at war was very distracting to the organisation and I could see it was very damaging to Telecom in the eyes of the public.

Chapter seven

telecom's dilemma

Telecommunications is a funny game because incumbent telcos in deregulated markets, wherever they are in the world, are essentially asked to perform an unnatural act. They are asked to work their hardest and smartest in the best interests of shareholders, which can only be done through providing superior services to customers, yet at the same time they are required to let their competitors access parts of their infrastructure to try to win those same customers. While I didn't see telecommunications as a zero-sum game — i.e. any competitor's gain was always a Telecom loss — the market does have to be growing very strongly for competitor gains not to come at the incumbent's expense. That basic dynamic, which doesn't exist in other industries, is the cause of much tension, particularly in markets such as New Zealand and Australia where there was one dominant provider (Telecom in New Zealand and Telstra in Australia). All around the world at this time, incumbent telcos were in conflict with regulators who were trying to ensure that the incumbent granted 'fair' access to their infrastructure to competitors — to act against its very nature in terms of a duty to maximise shareholder returns. In New Zealand and Australia in particular the idea of fairness resonates very strongly.

Some people held the view that when Telecom was privatised it should only have been given rights to service provision, not ownership of what ought to have remained a publicly owned network infrastructure. Even today, nearly 20 years after privatisation, there is still debate about whether there should be structural separation into two wholly independent entities, a service company and a network company. However, at this time we were an integrated national company and this had led to some protracted and unpleasant wrangling with the new companies entering the market who needed access to Telecom's infrastructure to carry out their business.

In July 2000 we announced a major interconnection deal with Telstra New Zealand, which in February that year had purchased Saturn. And three months later, much to many people's surprise, we announced a one-year interconnection deal with Clear and settled outstanding legal disputes after what had been quite a rancorous history, including litigation throughout the 1990s.

Richard Dammery at Telecom and Rhoda Holmes, then at Clear but who later came to work for me at Telecom, were instrumental in getting that agreement through. They decided quite early on that they were committed to getting a deal done and that they would lead their teams to move on from the unhelpful baggage of the past and go after a win-win outcome. Roderick was overseas at the time and when I rang him to say that we'd signed an interconnection deal with Clear, he was amazed and very pleased.

In a way, the other telcos had the flipside of Telecom's dilemma. For the smaller telcos, was it better to secure the best deal they could commercially and get on with life, or to spend their time distracted by trying to change the way the industry operated? We all compromised to get those deals done. There was no regulator (or government minister) holding a gun at anybody's head — the deals were done in a genuine spirit of what would work best for the industry and customers, some of whom, of course, were customers of two or more companies.

But such constructive behaviour is not as newsworthy as turbulence, of course, and the national telco discussion was dominated by interactions between Telecom and i4Free, which was an internet service provider owned by Call Plus. I was gobsmacked at the amount of coverage this matter received and the speed with which it became such big news. Of course, Call Plus was milking it for all it was worth. When you're a small internet service provider, all publicity is good publicity. There is absolutely no doubt that i4Free won the public relations game, being the 'David' in the David and Goliath narrative, never mind that many years later — too many years later, in my opinion — the High Court ruled in Telecom's favour against the Commerce Commission, which had launched a case over Telecom's introduction of 0867. The rapid growth in internet traffic had two consequences which the 0867 service was designed to address. The first was a massively increased loading on Telecom's network, the second an adverse and growing imbalance in fees payable by Telecom to Clear under an agreement made in 1996 which had not anticipated the impact the internet would have on the telecoms industry.

We set up a system whereby as long as customers added the prefix 0867 to their modem set-up they were not charged for dialling up their ISP to use the internet, and we made the 0867 number range available to other network operators as long as they agreed the number was not covered by existing interconnection agreements. The Commerce Commission appealed the High Court decision, which found that Telecom did not have an anti-competitive purpose when it introduced the 0867 service, to the Court of Appeal and lost. I would be very surprised if more than a handful of people know that both courts ruled in Telecom's favour. By then the damage was well done.

People forgot the specifics very quickly — if indeed they were ever well understood, interconnection between networks being a fairly arcane subject at the best of times — but the subtext of Telecom bullying the little guy became deeply rooted and set the scene for what was to occur later in the debate around unbundling and regulation.

By 2000 the internet was completely pervasive, and I believed that Telecom's centre of gravity needed to shift to reflect this. One of the things I wanted to do was to shift data technologies from the status of being secondary to voice at Telecom to being front and centre. We didn't know exactly how things would play out with the growth of email, the internet and other data technologies in the Telecom network, but we knew that we were seeing a shift away from 'voice' (phone calls) being the centre of our business, and that it would never just be about the physical infrastructure: it would be about what people did over that infrastructure.

In March 2000 the opportunity came up to buy 6 per cent of INL, which controlled SKY Television, so we took it. During this time Roderick and I flew to Los Angeles to meet Lachlan Murdoch as News Ltd was a major shareholder in INL. In May, we increased our stake to 10 per cent, then in February 2001 an opportunity came up to buy a stake in SKY directly. We saw this as a good fit strategically. In Australia, satellite and cable TV channel Foxtel is jointly owned by Telstra and a group of media players, including News Corporation.

Buying into a TV network had always seemed a good model for us to follow. SKY had access to international programming through British network BSkyB and other suppliers which it was delivering to an ever-increasing number of homes in New Zealand. We also thought the investment would show a good return simply in monetary terms, notwithstanding any synergy benefits. Once we had bought into the company, Marko joined the SKY board and we spent years trying to develop a deep relationship with SKY to create something neither of us could do by ourselves, linking SKY's content with our broadband technologies. While we did offer bundled SKY/ Telecom packages which were popular with customers, ultimately we concluded that it wasn't going to be possible to get a bigger stake and turn it into a really successful joint endeavour, so we sold our shares at a considerable profit a few years later when that became obvious.

Because we believed that our business would become more and

more data-centric, and we anticipated that this would be led by the business market, I wanted to make the most of our alliance with EDS and Microsoft, which had been announced the previous year. I hired Jane Freeman, the very well-respected previous head of BankDirect, to head esolutions, an early attempt to position Telecom in the business market as a serious player in the IT space. Esolutions was slightly ahead of its time, but it was the precursor to a successful strategy to shift us from being seen primarily as a telco to being a major player in IT. At that stage I didn't know how we could transform ourselves into an IT company, but I knew that it was going to be necessary.

Back in 1999, before I was CEO, Telecom had secured 80 per cent of AAPT, the biggest of the smaller telcos in Australia. In early 2000 we decided this was not a sustainable position and in August that year we successfully bid for the rest of AAPT. The combination of my focus on data and the need to make the Australian business efficient led me to support Karen Devonshire, who was then Telecom's CIO, in her thrust to win the business of the Commonwealth Bank of Australia. We spent months on that bid, which culminated in Telecom winning a very large piece of outsourced IT and T (telecoms) business. It was almost too big for us to digest and clearly it wasn't an area that AAPT had any expertise in. We obviously did a good enough job though, as the original five-year contract was later renewed for a further period.

Throughout 2000, two other things were also front and centre. Labour's promised Fletcher Inquiry into Telecommunications ran most of the year, reporting back to the government in October. It recommended introducing an industry-specific regulator and more regulation around Telecom and telecommunications in general, heralding the start of quite an intensive negotiation process with the Labour–Alliance government. This wasn't without some wins, particularly when you consider that the Alliance's Laila Harré was the Associate Minister of Communications! We established that the Kiwi Share costs (the cost of servicing unprofitable, more remote areas that were guaranteed telephone service and a flat-rate, free-calling option no higher than the standard residential rate when Telecom was privatised) should be spread around all the telcos and not solely borne by Telecom. Contrary to popular belief, this was not about revenue generation. The amount of money involved was small in comparison to Telecom's overall business, but it was really important to us in principle that the other telcos felt the burden of the Kiwi Share. We felt that it would therefore be much more likely that an industry solution would ultimately be found to the vexed question of how to deal with the Kiwi Share in a data-driven world when people had come to expect flat-rate local voice calling, wherever in the country they lived. Successive governments have just found that too much of a political hot potato to touch, although this area is currently under review again.

The other big concern was the end of the tech bubble. Telecom's share price was up around all-time high levels of over $9.80 the day before my birthday in April 2000, then, along with other telco stocks worldwide, began its descent. By July and August 2000 there were already stories in the media talking about 'Theresa losing her sparkle', 'Gattung getting grief'[8] and so on, and the fact that the financial market had never welcomed my appointment was now coming through in spades. I felt that my back was against the wall from the middle of that year onwards, which only made me more determined to survive.

Throughout 2000, events in the business environment worked against Telecom. On February 24, 2000, when news broke that Telstra and Saturn were joining forces in New Zealand, Telecom shares had lost 46 cents in one morning. The new Australian company was called TelstraSaturn, with Jack Matthews, then chief executive of Saturn, as its chief executive. This was the day after the government announced the telecommunications inquiry and Trevor Mallard was reported as saying, 'There is a view on the part of the government that there does need to be some change.'[9]

At the height of the tech boom, in those few months early in 2000, we were working around the clock to see if we could increase value by spinning off either the mobile business or Xtra, the ISP business, into separate businesses to be listed on the stock market. However, the market was starting to fall by late April and there became less of a gap between the value of fixed-line telcos and other related telco stocks such as internet businesses. In any event, we were strongly of the view that Telecom's strength lay in its integrated nature. We believed that, over time, the boundaries between mobile and fixed line and between the traditional voice and internet businesses would become increasingly blurred, to the extent that splitting the company into various bits, which might seem logical at the time, could soon look very illogical. So we shelved plans to hive off various divisions into separate companies.

Some market analysts were critical of this and thought that we should have spun off the faster-growing parts of the business. In any event we would not have had time to get a sharemarket float away even if we had made a decision in those few months before the bursting of the bubble sent all tech stocks down, whether they were mobile or fixed-line companies.

As chief financial officer, Marko Bogoievski took a huge burden off me in terms of immediately stepping up to manage the whole investor relations area as soon as he started in May 2000. Throughout our time together, which lasted for seven years, we were a very compatible CEO/CFO team with a yin and yang-type balance to our personalities and ways of doing things. Marko is a gifted communicator and presents information to investors in a logical and compelling manner. Over the next several years he became very highly regarded by the financial community both onshore and offshore, and he had his choice of roles when he left Telecom six months after I did, becoming chief operating officer at Infratil. Over time I grew in confidence dealing with analysts and investors myself, through frequent meetings and trips, particularly to the United States. I ended up striking up good relationships with many of them over a period of years, with Marko's assistance.

Telecom was such a big proportion of the New Zealand stock market that, generally speaking, most fund managers in New Zealand were already market weight and were thus unlikely to buy significantly more shares, so we were always looking for new investors outside of New Zealand. Marko and I travelled frequently to meet with potential new investors, especially to Australia and the United States.

Despite fluctuations in the Telecom share price and the fact that most of our key investors did not live in either Australia or New Zealand, over time we built a very good reputation for communicating with investors. We won multiple awards, culminating in the Best Investor Relations by an Australasian Company award as voted by international investors in 2006.

Communicating with institutional investors and the media is a tricky business for CEOs. You must communicate any matter of material significance to the whole financial market at the same time. This sense of needing to be careful contributed to me often feeling as if I was between a rock and a hard place.

In November 2000 I very much enjoyed hosting the gathering which celebrated the lighting up of the $1.5 billion Southern Cross cable project, with a dawn ceremony on Takapuna Beach, where the cable comes onshore in New Zealand. The cable, owned 50 per cent by Telecom, 40 per cent by Australian company Optus and 10 per cent by America's MCI WorldCom, had been an investment we'd approved a couple of years earlier to provide 120 times the capacity of the existing link between Australasia and North America. At a time when the market was growing so quickly, especially in terms of data loads, we were very glad of the increased capacity.

However, the year ended on a bit of a downer with the Telecom share price hitting a five-year low, dipping under $5.

Chapter eight

growing pains

The Telecom share price tracked strongly upwards for the first few months of 2001, then moved just as strongly downwards for most of the rest of the year. It is hard to overstate the pressure that a low or declining share price places on a company's CEO. Fund managers are themselves measured quarterly on the performance of their portfolios, and although some do see the long-term picture, all their incentives are based on performance over relatively short-term durations. As they see themselves as 'backing' you, they can become very angry and quite aggressive if your share price doesn't perform.

Aside from any major external factors taking the attention of the board, the amount of pressure on a CEO of a company listed on the stock market at any one time will tend to be directly related to how the company's share price is doing relative to its historical performance and to the market's expectations. Analysts are forever writing reports on companies and while they tend to use quite moderate language in their publications, you know that privately they'll be using much stronger language. Feedback can come directly or through what they say to the media, which is then reported.

Business analysis is a way of life for those involved in it and can seem to be a complete mystery, or at the very least a secret code, to those who are not. Journalists seek comment from financial analysts all the time, and often they'll take at face value what a person in the financial community says and make it part of the story, or even *the* story. Sometimes, although not always, what that person says can be motivated by whether they are 'long' or 'short' on the stock (in other words, whether their company has a financial interest in the share price going up or down).

Now, I don't have a problem with market participants having a particular view or particular take on a company's prospects, as long as it's made clear to the readers that they do in fact have an agenda and are not simply an informed, neutral observer. In the interests of complete disclosure, it would be more transparent if, whenever a broker or fund manager or analyst was quoted by a journalist, they had to say whether or not they were holders of the stock, as financial columnists have to do, and also whether their current recommendation to clients was hold, buy or sell. That would give the reader a better all-round perspective of the context of their remarks.

After its dip through mid-2001, Telecom's share price tracked upwards again particularly through 2003 and 2004 and held that level during 2005. The share price settled above $6 and, in combination with good dividends paid out over that period, it turned out that investors who had bought at the lows in late 2000 or 2001 had done quite well. It is no coincidence that positive reviews about my tenure as CEO coincided with this period during 2004 and 2005 when returns were seen to have been very good.

Over my time as CEO, I was annually issued stock options, as were other senior executives. Throughout 2003, 2004 and 2005 there were times when I could have profitably sold equity I had received in earlier periods but I never did this. Once I became CEO, I never sold any Telecom stock, because I strongly believed in the future of the company. Clearly it's not right for a CEO to be encouraging other investors to come on board if they don't strongly believe in the company's prospects for increased profitability. Even at times when I had no 'inside' information and I could have traded, I knew that it would not be a good look if relevant information subsequently emerged which could possibly be linked back to that time, even though I hadn't been aware of it then.

Anyway, Marko Bogoievski and I agreed quite early on in our working together that neither of us would sell any stock until after we had left Telecom. We were often talking to investors on different continents at the same time and had to totally trust each other, knowing that neither of us would do anything that would put the other in a difficult position. And it meant I could always sleep at night.

For much of 2001 I was quite focused on developments in Australia. UK company Cable & Wireless had announced they were selling Optus, the number two player in the Australian market behind Telstra. (AAPT, our company, was number three.) AAPT was a fixed-line business with no mobile business, which at that time was the fastest growing part of telecommunications worldwide. We spent some considerable time exploring alternatives to buy some or all of the Optus business in order to get a foothold in the Australian mobile market. I flew to Japan to meet with NTT DoCoMo, Japan's major telecommunications company, which at first was interested in a joint bid but later cooled on the idea. I also flew to Singapore with Marko to meet with SingTel, Singapore's major telecommunications company, which until that time had not shown its hand in terms of signalling whether or not they were interested in buying Optus. We warned the Telecom board that our interest might well help persuade SingTel that Optus was an asset worth having without any need to partner with us in procuring it. And that is exactly what happened.

Buying into Optus was always going to be a big stretch for us, so it was never a 'take no prisoners, this is the only option' situation. But it did make us more mindful of the perennial dilemma: Telecom is big by New Zealand standards but small by regional standards, let alone global standards. And it made us more focused on thinking about how we could work with what we had to both preserve existing revenue streams and grow parts of the business.

But first we had some unfinished business. Telecom had previously tried to buy into SKY TV in the mid 1990s and in February 2001 when an opportunity came up to buy in the board took the chance with enthusiasm. As I've said, it didn't turn out quite the way we hoped, but we still sold our shares some years later for a handsome profit.

With SingTel buying Optus and big IT companies joining forces in our region with media companies such as nineMSN, we could see that we would need regional alliances to avoid becoming isolated. We combined Xtra, our highly successful internet service provider, with Microsoft's MSN to create the XtraMSN portal. This was accompanied by Microsoft making a $300 million investment in Telecom through a convertible note issue.

In terms of mobile phones, we desperately needed to move from the 025 network, with its very limited capabilities. All over the world analogue networks, including the world's biggest, AT&T, were being phased out and handsets were no longer being produced. As nothing about technology stands still, we believed it was very important to get a third-generation product to market at speed. We knew there would be a choice of paths to whatever the next-generation technology was: we went with CDMA mobile technology for our network, partly because CDMA was the major technology used for mobile communications in North America, including by one of our then owners, Bell Atlantic, and it was popular throughout Asia, but also because we did not have a licence for GSM, which had a higher number of subscribers worldwide. (In fact, Telecom originally did have a licence for GSM some years before I joined, as did Bell South, which was later bought by Vodafone. I understood from Roderick that the government had required Telecom to sell its licence due to the view that it wouldn't be good for competition for the two main players to be on the same technology.)

At the time Telstra in Australia also had a nationwide CDMA network and in May 2001 we announced a roaming agreement with Telstra enabling Telecom mobile customers to use their phones in Australia. This helped our sales considerably, as we were being walloped by Vodafone in terms of global roaming capability because their phones could be used in the many more countries which were also on GSM.

We announced a mobile deal in Australia with Hutchison, a large Asian telco which had a presence in Australia. It was a complex deal, but it basically amounted to Hutchison selling us their 3G (third-generation, essentially mobile broadband) mobile phone licence and spectrum in Australia. At the time the Australian media saw it as a good deal, considering that European companies had forked out more than $240 billion for 3G mobile licences in the previous couple of years. Shares in both Telecom and Hutchison rose after the announcement.

In 2001 our investment in the Southern Cross cable also started to pay off, when a $220 million dividend from Southern Cross put a shine on our third-quarter results announced that May.

So we got a lot done in 2001 and it had felt like a great adventure. There was a real sense that momentum was coming back into the company. However, the telco mantra of growth, which had been on everyone's lips through 1999 and 2000, had by now been replaced with one of 'keep costs under control and grow your revenue faster than your expenses', in the wake of the tech bubble bursting. In other words, boring is good.

In November the deal that had been rumoured all year was finally sealed: TelstraSaturn bought Clear Communications for $435 million and Jack Matthews, TelstraSaturn's chief executive, was replaced by Rosemary Howard from Telstra Australia. No sooner had Rosemary turned up in New Zealand than the media were playing up the so-called 'battle of the broads'[10]. The media was fascinated by the fact the two largest telcos in New Zealand were both headed up by women. I didn't find Rosemary easy to deal with — she put me on edge — but it was probably mutual!

Some years earlier, when I was having a problem dealing with a woman who was at the same level as me at Telecom, a male colleague suggested to me that I might like to have a look in the mirror. He thought that after so many years in a largely male corporate environment, my style was adapted to work effectively with men but not particularly effectively with women, or not with women who didn't report to me, anyway! Given my very strong pro-women perspective and the time and money I had put into women's causes over the years and into mentoring individual women, it was quite a shock to be challenged like that. But it did make me reflect on whether, in fact, I had my own 'queen bee' syndrome going on, in that I would happily share power or share the limelight with men, but was much more uncomfortable doing so with other women.

Of course, there have been many women I have enjoyed working with, such as Patsy Reddy, who was on the Telecom board while I was chief executive. I found her to be diligent, thoughtful about the issues and considered in her approach. Over time I developed an innate sense about high-powered women in corporate environments and whether they were male-identified in their style and tended to think there was room for only a few, perhaps a *very* few, women at the top — perhaps just them — or whether they were supportive of other women. Interestingly, I never could figure out where Rosemary fitted in this characterisation.

By mid-2002 Rosemary was in full flight arguing Telstra's case for greater regulation of Telecom. Eventually she and I finally sorted out the Telecom and TelstraClear interconnection and billing issues — including billing disagreements dating back as far as 1996 — and announced a commercial interconnect deal that August. It felt good to have tidied all that up.

In late 2001, Douglas Webb was made Telecommunications Commissioner at the Commerce Commission. Now there was a regulator who had the final say on matters such as interconnection. Douglas struck me as a careful, measured person and at the time I didn't have a strong view as to whether or not having a regulator was going to have a strong impact on us.

In January 2002 I made changes to the management team that would become pivotal. I shrank the executive team from 12 people to eight, because I felt it would be much easier with a smaller group of people to get alignment of vision, a high degree of trust and strong collegial relationships to role-model to the rest of the organisation.

Of that group, Marko Bogoievski (chief financial officer), Mark Ratcliffe (chief information officer), Mark Verbiest (group general counsel) and Simon Moutter (chief operating officer) made up the heart of the executive team with me until I left Telecom in June 2007.

I promoted Simon to the new role of chief operating officer for the New Zealand business, thus aligning the sales and service division with the network division, which he had previously led. I believed that one person having end-to-end accountability would be the best way to deal with tensions between the two sides of the business, which had been endemic in Telecom ever since I'd been there. People in the network operations area and those who are selling and marketing telecommunications products seem to have very different DNA! In Simon I recognised a very effective business-unit manager whom I believed would be able to bring the two areas together and make the total greater than the sum of the individual pieces. Simon proved to be highly effective, and when he left Telecom, a year after I did, he went on to become chief executive of Auckland International Airport.

It is not unusual for CEOs to engender loyalty in their immediate executive team and for the people who report to them to be committed to the organisation and to them personally. It is more unusual for the top management team to be as committed to each other. This is what I strove to achieve and believe that I did. Even under times of great stress, we held together as a team and supported each other.

This didn't mean we always agreed — far from it. In particular Simon, who tends to be a very pragmatic, goal-oriented leader, and Marko, who thinks longer term and more strategically, often came at issues from different angles. But great confidence in each person's core competencies, and respect for their contributions, created a very harmonious leadership group. (In fact, in 2002 there was a small piece in an Australian newspaper which suggested there was a rift in the executive team. In response, Marko was quoted as saying the story was so off-beam it was embarrassing to print and that he couldn't imagine a more aligned team.[11])

I think that playing politics in an organisation, whether a business or otherwise, is insidiously destructive. I believe that reasonable people can, when presented with the same facts, come to different conclusions about what's the best thing to do, and how best to get there, but that's to be expected. After my experience with some of my colleagues during my five years at Telecom before becoming CEO, I resolved to never again put myself in a situation where I was working with people more concerned about their own egos than the needs of the organisation.

Not long after I made these changes, in February 2002, we reported our quarterly result to the market, which was better than expected with earnings per share up 10 per cent on a year earlier. Operating earnings (EBITDA) had increased in both the New Zealand and Australian businesses and analysts heralded the result as very impressive. In the previous year we had generated sequential quarterly increases on EBITDA: a year-on-year increase of 3.4 per cent in the June 2001 quarter, a 5 per cent increase in the September quarter, and a 12.7 per cent increase in the December quarter. *The Independent* reported that Telecom was probably the top performing company worldwide in our sector for the half year to December,[12] and in June London consultants IR Group named Telecom the world's best performer in the global telecommunications sector.[13] I was as pleased as Punch.

The December 2001 half year was followed by another good few months to March 2002, in which we again beat analysts' predictions. This marked 11 quarters in a row where our margins and operating performance had improved. At the full year's financial results in August we wrote down the value of AAPT, but the market liked the 9 per cent growth in underlying annual earnings and the share price rose.

Telecom had purchased AAPT in 1999 at what looked like a

good price at that time, reported as such by the Australian media. Importantly, due to hard work under the leadership of David Bedford, who had gone there at my request to head up that business, we were able to announce that the Australian business was cashflow positive, although not yet showing a profit on the investment to date.

In the boom times, the market had encouraged telcos to borrow substantially to engage in takeover activity and spend huge sums on buying new technology. Following the global high-tech meltdown, however, this had all changed as global telco share prices sank and rating agencies changed their views. Suddenly debt was bad. The priority shifted towards cost-cutting to reduce debt and an emphasis on cashflow and earnings growth. And we had responded quickly to the new rules. We startled analysts by announcing the Australian business was cashflow positive for the first time, up to two years earlier than many analysts had expected. While a couple of years earlier we had been focused on growth, we had always been conservative in terms of our balance sheet and protective of our strong credit rating. Roderick in particular was a stickler for making sure that the company could ride out any market downturn in good shape, and I was determined to carry that on. Overall, operating earnings in Australia as measured by EBITDA improved 47 per cent in the full year 2002.

We were strongly focused on improving our underlying core business in both countries during 2002. The year was one of lowering costs, improving yields, containing capital spending and retiring debt, all of which drew congratulatory media from the financial community, but none of which endeared Telecom to the general public.

In May 2002, the Prime Minister's office asked me to lead a business delegation to Australia for the first trans-Tasman combined business and government visit for some considerable time. Of course I said yes and cancelled plans to visit investors overseas, asking Marko to go instead, so that I could accompany Helen Clark on that trip. It was my first opportunity to be up close to her for a period of time and it was eye-opening in many ways. It was impossible not to be impressed with her grasp of issues, both in a broad sense and at a detailed level, and her huge stamina in that whirlwind of a week. However, I was astonished by the way officials talked to her. The level of deference was something I've never seen exhibited in business.

In late September 2002, Verizon, formerly Bell Atlantic, sold their remaining 20 per cent stake in Telecom. What this meant was that Telecom no longer had a stable cornerstone investor. It was now owned by fund managers across the globe, but particularly in America and Australia. There were about 50,000 investors in New Zealand and about the same number in the United States, with none of those individuals having a significant stake. So the company's share price would be driven even more by how offshore fund managers viewed its likely future growth and profitability.

I love New Zealand and I admire and enjoy America, and can easily move back and forth between the two countries. By New Zealand standards, I have quite a big personality but not by American ones! Still, if you are American, especially a New Yorker who has never been to New Zealand, or a Kiwi who's never spent very much time in America, understanding the mores of the two cultures can be a bit like explaining colour to someone born blind. Perhaps because we look alike and we speak the same language, we are more inclined to fail to see the dissimilarities between the two countries. But Telecom, a former public utility, now a private company owned by return-oriented investors from the US northeast, was always likely to run smack into enshrined Kiwi notions of playing the game fairly being more important than winning, and putting people and services before profit. And eventually it did.

November 2002 proved to be a very tumultuous month. For some time we had been exploring ways to reduce costs and increase revenues in the core business in New Zealand (although we didn't think of taking away post-paid envelopes and making customers buy their own stamps when they were paying their bills — it took another Telecom management team to come up with that, some years later!). We decided that we needed to recover some of the costs of connecting people in very remote areas and so announced a policy of charging one-third of the cost of the actual connection in high-cost-to-service areas. This represented quite an increase for the 1000 or 2000 customers a year affected by the new policy, who had previously been paying a mere fraction of the actual cost. We thought this policy was reasonable — it was nowhere near the full cost recovery which other utilities sought — but a furore ensued. It was huge news and certain government ministers were apoplectic.

I went to a meeting at the Beehive chaired by Jim Anderton where I thought one of his colleagues was going to spit at me, he was literally foaming at the mouth so much. Jim chaired that meeting very effectively, pointing out to his colleagues that they had been part of a government that had sold Telecom back in the 1990s (when he had opposed the sale), and given that they had sold it, they could no longer tell it what to do. Eventually we hammered out a compromise position, charging more than we had previously done, but less than we originally intended. I will never forget walking out of that meeting to be greeted by a huge barrage of reporters.

In this same week we realised that although our full-year profit would meet the market's expectations, the quarter we were about to report would not. Under the continuous disclosure rules we had to let the market know that their consensus expectations were too high, which we promptly did. Predictably, the share price took a dive, and Marko and I cancelled our planned trip to the Melbourne Cup. Having a good time was the last thing on our minds.

Finally, Telecommunications Commissioner Douglas Webb gave his first ruling on rates for network interconnection. I was very annoyed at his decision to set the interconnection price Telecom could charge other networks for accessing its infrastructure at 1.13 cents per minute, because it was lower than the initial draft decision of 1.21–1.42 cents per minute which Douglas had indicated a few months earlier. I pointed out that there had been no point in publishing a range of estimates if we weren't able to rely on the final decision being within that range.

Clearly the interconnection decision, the tumult over rural connection charges and the profit warning all came together in an ugly confection of events. It didn't take some media long to speculate about whether I would keep my job — barely a few months after I had been lauded as having the company in great shape, with world-beating telco-sector performance!

However, when we announced the quarter's profit and the market could see that underlying earnings actually grew 8 per cent year-on-year for the quarter, some of the frenzy died down. Indeed, EBITDA had grown every year I was CEO, from $1.96 billion in 1999 to $2.26 billion by June 2002, an average of more than 5 per cent per year. As one or two commentators had noted, not too many telcos around the world could claim as much in the tough environment of those years.[14]

Predictably, after that rather bad-hair week, Roderick was asked whether my job was under threat. He was quoted as saying, 'the board has been very satisfied with the performance of the management team and has total confidence in Theresa as chief executive. My endorsement is straightforward and unequivocal and I can guarantee you it's shared by all of my board colleagues.'[15] I really appreciated his support. But it is always very interesting to speculate about people, and when we presented the half-year result together in February 2003 a journalist on the conference call asked me if I felt pressured by speculation over my job security.

Roderick responded that while the telecommunications sector was hugely demanding, Telecom was in a strong state with unusually strong cashflow and debt repayment ahead of schedule, and that the board was more than satisfied with management. That still did not stop the question being asked again to my face by a journalist later in the day. I laughed — as I often did at such questions — and Simon Moutter, ever loyal and always prepared to stand up for what or who he believed in, sprang to my defence, saying that the attacks were ridiculous and needed to end. Pressed again, I pointed out that no telco CEO was having rose petals strewn in their path — which I thought was rather a good answer.

In hindsight, the rural connection issue reflected a huge conflict between Telecom being a big, publicly listed company answerable to its shareholders and a public perception that it still had some wider social role, an overhang of telephones being seen as a social service or Telecom's previous government ownership. I pointed out during the rural connection fees debate that if you saw a Telstra van in rural New Zealand, it was probably lost. (Actually I appropriated this from Ziggy Switkowski, Telstra's CEO, who used the same line in Australia to take a shot at Optus, so thanks for the quote, Ziggy!) I thought it was very funny and, like all good humour, it contained more than a kernel of truth — unlike us, our rivals didn't have to service rural areas so they didn't.

Chapter nine

the big issues

In February 2003 David Bedford, who had been running the Australian business, decided that he would retire, as he really wanted to come back to New Zealand. David had done a great job bringing much greater financial discipline into AAPT that had enabled us to turn that operation to cashflow-positive status, thereby contributing cash to the group, much faster than many people had expected. Marko was passionate about the potential of the Australian business and we decided that the best thing would be for him to run AAPT (while continuing to be Telecom's chief financial officer) while we searched for David's replacement. I was strongly of the view that an Australian should run the company, but I was open-minded about what background they should come from. With the benefit of hindsight, I think it was a mistake to ask Marko to both run AAPT and be CFO. He is one of the most dedicated and hard-working executives I've ever worked with, but by the end of this stint even his reserves of stamina were depleted.

Trisha McEwan had joined my team as head of human resources early in 2002. I had tried to hire Trisha back in 2000, but at that stage she was head of human resources at Fletchers and was committed to finishing her work there before joining an Australian consulting firm. I had better luck attracting her second time around! Trisha, whose brother is the Saatchi & Saatchi chief Kevin Roberts, was and is a very savvy and effective HR practitioner, highly regarded across Australia and New Zealand, but even with her on board we struggled to find the right person to lead AAPT.

Although we got some early traction under the leadership of new CEO Jon Stretch, an experienced Australian IT executive, the problems with the business were structural, relating to Telstra's dominance in the market, rather than executional. At that time AAPT was a distant number three in the Australian telecommunications market and Telstra was still majority owned (51.8 per cent) by the Australian government. Despite Rosemary Howard's claims when she came to New Zealand that Telstra in Australia was much better for its competitors to deal with than Telecom was in New Zealand, that was not our experience. Still, the management team circa 2003 looked like paragons of reasonableness compared to our later experience when Sol Trujillo turned up to run Telstra.

Meanwhile, back in New Zealand it was all about the right strategies and people to drive the business forward. Saatchi & Saatchi had long held the Telecom advertising account — indeed, it was the jewel in the crown for the New Zealand business and the Wellington office of Saatchi & Saatchi in particular. For close to a decade I'd enjoyed a good relationship with James Hall, for many years the general manager of Saatchi & Saatchi in Wellington, although our relationship pre-dated that as he was the BNZ account director when I was chief manager – marketing for the bank in the early 1990s (at that stage he was at Colenso). He took up Kevin Roberts's challenge to leave New Zealand and run Saatchi in the UK, based in London. However, after a short time there, there was a dust-up which turned into a bust-up, and James left Saatchis and returned home to join forces with a few other ex-Saatchi Wellington mates of his in an agency called Assignment. I thought James was a terrific advertising guy and he had been a passionate extended member of my marketing team. After he arrived back in New Zealand in early 2004 he called me up and basically said, 'Well, I'm back, when do we start working for Telecom?'

I had to choose between Saatchi & Saatchi and Kevin Roberts, their global head who I'd first met when he became worldwide CEO of Saatchi a couple of years earlier, and who I had found to be one of the smartest and most visionary people I'd ever dealt with, and James and a small boutique agency. I backed Kevin and chose to stay with Saatchi. After what had been a bit of a dry patch, Kevin hired Andrew Stone to head the Saatchi New Zealand business, and Saatchi went on to make some great ads for Telecom. Ironically, Assignment went on to pick up the TelstraClear advertising account.

After a difficult second quarter at the end of 2002, the third quarter (the first calendar quarter of 2003) was strong, and we reported earnings of just under $200 million. This was 11 per cent up on normalised earnings for the same period the previous year and beat the market's profit expectations. Our focus on cutting debt and carefully managing capital spending to boost our cashflows won friends in the financial community, and Telecom's share price tracked steadily upwards during the rest of 2003. And sure enough, the media commentary about my performance became much more positive too. I breathed a huge sigh of relief and started to relax a bit.

One of the more enjoyable things I got to do in 2003 was take up the invitation to attend the Bill Gates International CEO Summit in Seattle in June that year. I was invited regularly in my years as CEO but I was able to go only twice. That year we were able to try out the first generation of tablet PCs, which was great fun.

It was an amazing experience to go to these summits but, not surprisingly, both times I attended there were only a few women. It was there that I met Carly Fiorina, at that stage CEO of Hewlett

Packard; Meg Whitman, then CEO of eBay; and Carol Bartz, then CEO of Autodesk and now CEO of Yahoo!. And, of course, I met many CEOs who I'd only previously read about. Warren Buffett proved as entertaining and wise in person as I'd anticipated, and all the CEO panel sessions were very interesting. I was asked to join Bill Gates, Warren Buffett and several of the CEOs in a press conference at the event, which I was happy to do.

I had met Bill in my first week as CEO of Telecom, on a trip with the board to visit Microsoft and other tech companies in the United States. Bill in person is exactly as you would imagine him to be based on the Bill the world sees in virtual mode — intense, with intelligence to burn, and very action-oriented. His home, which he shares with his wife Melinda and family, was large, but it was tasteful and very much a home, not a showpiece. But of course not everybody has security guards in their garden!

For me the most remarkable features of the house were the dining room, where 100 CEOs comfortably had dinner together, and the screen in the dining room which could flick backwards and forwards from exactly replicating the view outside the house to any other image that we wanted to see. But the most amazing room, or should I say series of rooms, was the library. Looking at the originals of some of the great documents of American history and historic letters that I had never previously seen was fantastic, and I could easily have spent weeks in there.

As an aside, I have also met 'the other Bill', both times in New Zealand. I twice had one-on-one sessions with Bill Clinton, the first time when he was still US President, in September 1999, when he visited New Zealand for APEC, and the second time post-presidency, when he visited Auckland on his world speaking tour in 2006. It's true what they say about his charisma: for the nanoseconds that he is talking to you and focused on you, you feel completely captivated — and then he's gone and on to the next person. Both times he spoke well and I felt his speech in 2006 particularly showed a deep understanding of other countries' challenges.

My other connection with Bill Clinton was that I was with Peri Drysdale in Australia in 2002 when she was rung and told that Bill had walked into one of her stores and purchased a garment. To say she was thrilled was an understatement! This was a great reward for Peri's hard efforts over many years running Snowy Peak and Untouched World, promoting the best of New Zealand's natural merino wool and possum products and a range of clothing and lifestyle items.

Meanwhile, back at home TelstraClear was adopting an increasingly aggressive stance. The price set by the Telecommunications Commissioner for interconnection was a much better deal for TelstraClear than anyone was expecting. Nevertheless, Rosemary Howard thought the deal wasn't good enough and appealed against it. In June, at a telecommunications summit in Auckland, I challenged her to drop Telstra's appeals to the Commerce Commission and in return we would abandon the counter appeals which we had lodged to protect our interests. I pointed out that the whole thing was rather counterproductive but TelstraClear was not prepared to negotiate. There was much mirth among a few journalists when Rosemary and I sat together on the panel discussion at that event as we were dressed almost identically in dark pin-striped suits and pearl necklaces.

In New Zealand we carried on down the path of outsourcing deals and improving efficiency in the company. We outsourced the supply and management of our new 027 mobile network to Lucent, who'd built the network 18 months previously. And we outsourced the management of the New Zealand fixed line network to Alcatel.

Telecom had always had strong support from investors in the United States but very little support in Australia. Mark Flesher, general manager – investor relations, Marko Bogoievski and I had worked hard at trying to get Australian fund managers interested in buying the stock, and in the 12 months to the middle of 2003 the proportion of stock owned by Australian institutions more than doubled. By April 2003 Australian institutions owned 16 per cent of Telecom, up from 7 per cent in April 2002. The growing presence of

Australian companies on Telecom New Zealand's share register was in many cases at the expense of Telstra, as during the year our share price had climbed while Telstra's had fallen.

The good financial result for the three months to March 2003 was followed up by another good result for the three months to the end of June, where we saw both a recovery in revenue growth and the benefits of cutting costs. Australia was now comfortably cashflow positive, contributing $92 million cash to the group result, compared with negative $28 million the previous year.

On the back of a good result, most analysts increased their profit forecasts for the following year. That's the trouble when you deliver good results — the bar gets raised ever higher.

My biggest worry at that time in the New Zealand business was mobile. Although we had delivered the new 027 network on time and on budget, we were still clearly underperforming Vodafone and, in particular, we were weak in the youth market. Telecom was simply not as 'cool' as Vodafone. When I saw that Greg Muir was leaving as the CEO of The Warehouse I called him immediately to see if I could hire him on a short-term contract to help us focus on marketing and merchandising mobile at the retail level. Simon Moutter and I had already convinced one of our most talented general managers, Kevin Kenrick, to take on the challenge of improving mobile performance, and he worked with Greg on developing an action plan that dramatically changed the game.

One of the things we'd been working on for some time was trying to accelerate the shift of customers from our old 025 network onto 027. The mobile team came up with the brainwave of offering unlimited texting for $10 per month and we launched $10 a month 'all you can text' in August 2003.

At the time we launched $10 texting, 63 per cent of our 027 customers were texters. On average they spent $8 per month on text messages. But among those who texted, 20 per cent sent more than two texts per day, and of course there was a group of very heavy users sending as many 3000 text messages per month, so they stood to save heaps. Given that many of the heavy texters were teenagers, the combination of $10 texting and our souped-up advertising turned Telecom Mobile from their parents' mobile company into a real contender for their business. Vodafone didn't match our offering, instead responding with an essentially two-for-one offer, i.e. buy $40 of prepaid air time and we will double it.

Our initiative proved to be a real winner with customers and completely changed the game in mobile. Indeed, Telecom's 027 service was voted Mobile Service of the Year at the TUANZ (Telecommunications Users Association of New Zealand) Awards for the second year running.

We had worked hard all year, with regular performance reviews of every part of the business, and we were growing earnings, but it was really difficult to address the really big, fundamental issues about telecommunications that were the same around the world. Technology was always driving down the price by providing customers with cheaper alternatives, so it was very hard to grow top-line revenues. Nevertheless, the market responded to the immediate improvement in financial results, and the Australian media ran headlines like 'Telecom New Zealand in sparkling form'[16].

On September 18, 2003 the Telecommunications Commissioner released his draft decision on unbundling of the local loop, i.e. that rival telcos should be able to put their equipment into Telecom exchanges and plug into our network, thereby avoiding having to invest in core network themselves. Rosemary Howard was very upbeat about this and actually called it an exciting decision. Me, I thought that most Kiwis weren't particularly interested in unbundling per se, although they did want to see competitors given a fair go. The arguments in favour of unbundling were fairly easy to mount and the ones against more complex, but whichever way we looked at it, we knew it was going to be bad news for us. I was very determined to try and reverse the draft decision although very few people at Telecom believed this would be possible.

Also about this time, the first commentary started to appear in the media about New Zealand being well down the developed country rankings for broadband and linking the slow uptake to Telecom. Throughout 2003 I had many meetings with a variety of cabinet ministers, including the Minister of Communications, Paul Swain, who was a decent bloke and pretty straightforward to deal with. The meetings were about different topics, from the possibility of jamming cellphone coverage in prisons through how to improve broadband penetration in rural New Zealand. Interestingly, at none of these meetings did any cabinet minister ever say to me, 'We think you, Telecom, should be doing more about broadband'.

In 2003 I'd been invited to join the government's Growth and Innovation Advisory Board, which again led to lots of interaction with cabinet ministers. Once more, there was plenty of opportunity to say to me either formally or informally, 'Hey, we think you should be doing more in this area'. At no stage did this happen. Later it was repeated ad nauseam that the government had warned Telecom many times about broadband. In fact, I'm not sure that anyone from the government ever claimed they had — it just seemed to be asserted, then repeated and accepted as a fact.

One of the positive things we were doing with broadband was the introduction of Coronet, a video-conferencing network between secondary schools. In September I went to Te Aroha College in the Waikato for a demonstration of the system, with Helen Clark. (This was the second time we had done a schools broadband visit together; we had earlier gone down to Dunedin, where ex-MP Clive Mathewson had been an early mover behind getting Otago schools hooked up to broadband.) There, schools were using broadband to offer a greater range of subjects to students than was otherwise possible at smaller schools outside the bigger cities.

In early September 2003 we had a fantastic leadership day for the top 100 leaders and influencers in the company. My direct reports recommended who in their team should attend and I made the final call. It was a chance for me to openly discuss what I thought I had done well and what mistakes I had made in the previous few years.

People weren't used to a chief executive who admitted they were fallible and it sent a strong message about the candour I expected from everyone.

I spoke in Hamilton at a business luncheon in late 2003 and a reporter who interviewed me noted that I was walking around carrying a tattered pair of comfortable shoes in my briefcase, which I regularly did because I can't walk far in high heels without getting a sore back and besides, you can't move fast enough in them! She thought it said something about how comfortable I was in my job, which was true, although I actually carried all sorts of things round in my briefcase, including a random assortment of food. Philip King, at the time investor relations manager, remembers driving around London with me pulling marmalade sandwiches out of my briefcase between meetings!

trouble on the home front

If 2003 was a very good year for me workwise, it was about to turn into a very bad year for me personally. On Monday, October 6, when I arrived home from work, John told me he was unhappy and was considering leaving. This wasn't the first time.

Throughout my first years as Telecom CEO, John was hugely supportive, both practically — doing most of the shopping and all of the cooking — and emotionally. In fact, his support of me had never wavered from the time we met as university students in Hamilton. We were intellectually very compatible and enjoyed a deep emotional resonance. He was a pillar of support for me.

During 2000, my first year in the job, he himself was in transition, having decided that after 15 years of being a successful economist it was time to do something more creative. Throughout that year he compiled a photography portfolio, then in 2001 he started his first year at photography school.

During the course of that year a distance started to emerge between us. I was totally consumed with my job; indeed, I had been so busy that I'd hardly noticed when John didn't remember my birthday in April. One day in November 2001 he had called me at work, late on a Friday, and said he'd prepared something for me. I came home to an array of interesting, creatively assembled presents and a very belated birthday card. I was touched by the effort he'd gone to.

At the time I didn't give much thought to the impact on my relationship of putting so much into my work. I've always understood that you can't go home and cuddle a briefcase and thought I'd always successfully balanced my work and relationship. But I'm a 'full-on' person and, looking back, I can see it must have been very difficult for John. There were three of us in the 'marriage' alright — me, him and my job.

Just before my fortieth birthday, in April 2002, he had told me for the first time that he was not happy in the relationship and wondered if we should separate. I was completely shocked. Chris Woodwiss, my highly competent executive assistant who had become a good friend, was organising a special party for me so the show had to go on. John gave a wonderful speech — a tribute to me and our time together — and put together a lovely book of photos of my life, but I felt emotionally discombobulated all evening. Friends had travelled from around the country to be there, but it was not quite the joyful event I had anticipated. John's words seemed to have come so out of the blue. Things settled down again between us, but in hindsight it was a warning signal I didn't heed closely enough.

As part of our commitment to restoring our relationship, John and I hired a convertible and spent a week in May 2003 driving the Californian coast road from Los Angeles to San Francisco. It was a spectacular drive which he'd always wanted to do, and it reinforced my positive feelings about California in general and the Carmel –Monterey area in particular. I like the climate, the majesty of the rugged coastline and the energy of the area — simultaneously vibrant and relaxed. We had a nice time and I missed him when he went back to New Zealand as I stayed on in the United States a bit longer for work reasons.

When matters came to a head again a few months later I was shocked. John was so down, so emotionally flat. I knew that we hadn't been as connected in the past year or so but I just assumed that we would work things through, which is what I told him. I had no intention of leaving him. Despite being resolute that our relationship could be saved, I was very upset — I went and had a bath and cried. We'd been together for nearly 20 years at that point. Not only was he my partner, he was also my best friend, and I couldn't quite figure out how this had happened to us.

The life of a CEO is relentless. It makes no accommodation for times of personal travail or struggle. The next day, a Tuesday, I had to host a 'Be Your Best' day for high-achieving Telecom staff and then fly to Auckland that evening for a Telecom board meeting, a board rehearsal for the AGM on Wednesday evening, and the AGM itself on Thursday. I had a great deal of difficulty putting my personal life to the back of my mind so I could get through everything.

Chris Woodwiss immediately realised something was wrong when she saw me, and when we got to Auckland she came to my hotel room. I burst into tears and told her what John had said. However, I had no choice but to pull myself together and go off to the meeting, the rehearsal and then front a stormy AGM.

The three-hour AGM, attended by about 300 shareholders, was dominated by debate from the floor. The appointment to the board of previous BNZ boss Lindsay Pyne had turned out to be surprisingly controversial. I gave an interview a couple of weeks later and said the days around the AGM were not among my better ones, but no one who read the article would have understood quite why I was saying that. The words definitely had two meanings.

After John dropped his bombshell, work was a great source of routine and security to me. And there was a lot of work to focus on. We were particularly engaged in building on the $10 texting and improving the appeal of our mobile offerings to customers, as well as engaging with the Telecommunications Commissioner to try to get him to change his mind about recommending unbundling. Our argument was not that there was no need for the market to be competitive but that overseas, unbundling had not been the panacea that had been expected, with the number of unbundled lines miniscule in relation to the number of years unbundling had been common. We felt wholesaling of the network, which meant competitors could buy broadband services from Telecom and wouldn't have to install their own equipment in exchanges, would lead to much faster take-up by competitors and a much faster choice of broadband alternatives in the market for customers, because competitors wouldn't have to physically install equipment. I also consistently argued that the broadband debate was shaped by a PC-centric view of life that said that the fixed line was king and always would be, whereas customers were voting with their feet and adopting mobile in droves. Ultimately, mobile broadband would be what mattered the most.

The unbundling debate raged far and wide. Smaller competitors who had invested in wireless network infrastructure, such as Woosh, were lobbying the Telecommunications Commissioner, arguing that unbundling hadn't been effective in the United States. They also said that by unbundling, the regulator was effectively choosing a technology, in this case DSL (a technology used to transmit data digitally over the wires of the existing local telephone network), in a way that would set uneconomic prices and make it high risk for those companies which were actually building new network infrastructure and competing against others who were effectively piggybacking off Telecom's network infrastructure.

In December 2003, having heard all the submissions and reviewed the overseas evidence, Douglas Webb stunned the IT community by reversing his draft decision and recommending against unbundling. Instead, he recommended rigorous rules around wholesaling be applied to Telecom's provision of service to its competitors.

Although the commissioner's decision to recommend to the

government that it not unbundle the local loop surprised many, it was not without its supporters. In particular, the well-respected journalist and commentator Rod Oram had written a very reasoned piece shortly before the decision came out in which he looked at evidence from around the world. He concluded that the case was fairly finely balanced, but that putting in place a more regulated wholesale regime and waiting a couple of years to see how that played out alongside investment in other technologies from competing players was a perfectly reasonable approach.[17]

Aside from the unbundling debate, our focus in broadband throughout 2003 was mainly one of reach. About 65 per cent of Fonterra's farmers were beyond the reach of Telecom's fixed-line copper network for high-speed internet access and we were working hard to improve this through our partnership with state-owned transmission company Broadcast Communications Ltd (BCL), which we had entered into in July 2002, and through focused initiatives such as Fonterra Net.

Telecom underwrote the return to BCL (now called Kordia) on our partnership, which enabled the launch of BCL Extend to rural New Zealand. I met with Craig Boyce, then chair of BCL, and hammered out the final details of the deal. We knew when we looked at the business case that there was no way that Telecom would ever make money out of it: we did it because we wanted to help accelerate getting broadband out into rural New Zealand. But of course we could never do enough and even now, many years later, there are parts of New Zealand that are just not economic for broadband. I believe it has always been spurious to compare New Zealand's broadband take-up with that of densely populated countries in geographically confined areas. The main broadband issue in 2003 was not speed or price; it was the perceived digital divide, the fact that for large numbers of people living in rural New Zealand, dial-up was the only option.

Predictably, against a backdrop of improvements in business performance and a steadily rising share price, reports of my imminent demise disappeared. Interestingly though, at least one Australian

journalist who interviewed financial analysts around this time
reported that some of them believed improvements in the business
were largely due to chief operating officer Simon Moutter and chief
financial officer Marko Bogoievski, rather than myself!

A male CEO would have been applauded for hiring Marko and
promoting Simon. Instead, because I am a woman, it raised the
possibility that maybe I wasn't really running things at all. It's true
that Simon and Marko were both fantastic and both went on to major
CEO roles when they left Telecom, but there's no male CEO in the
world with a strong executive team who wouldn't be credited with
building that team and developing them so that they went on to greater
heights afterwards, and for selecting them in the first place. I never
have been and never will be challenged by having fantastic people
around me. During the previous few years stories had occasionally
strayed into 'Well, after all, she's not really running Telecom because
Roderick's still really running it. She's his protégé. He controls her.'
This time there was a similar theme, but it was about the men who
reported to me! But once again it illustrated that, by and large, we
have a very uneasy relationship with the notion of women in power.

winning
the battle . . .

In February 2004 we announced a $365 million profit for the second half of 2003, and a lift in the dividend from 5 cents to 7.5 cents a quarter. (These days, a few short years later, Telecom doesn't make much more profit than this in a whole year.) The financial result was 21 per cent up on the previous corresponding period and was buoyed by a $28 million part-payment from the sale of Telecom's 12 per cent stake in SKY Television. Broadband (Jetstream) customers had nearly doubled, to 90,000 from 54,000 the year before, and the rate of people converting from dial-up internet to broadband was also doubling.

The share price rocketed up all year, helped by the Commerce Commission's decision not to recommend unbundling to the government. We and our competitors then spent the early part of 2004 lobbying the government, especially the then Minister of Communications, Paul Swain, to make a decision on actioning the

Commission's recommendation.

I personally spent hours on this. I met with the minister to see if there was any way that we could get official or unofficial government endorsement of us setting a bold broadband target, but he refused to be drawn. He felt it was improper for the government to look anything other than 'hands off' in the matter. Given that the review of unbundling had become about how to get broadband out to more people more quickly, although the original focus had been more about fostering competition, I also wrote to the minister setting out our commitment to a goal of 250,000 households with broadband by the end of 2005, along with our view that a third of our projected growth in broadband would come from other players acting as wholesalers or resellers of Telecom's products.

However, the Ministry of Economic Development officials who advise the minister did not agree with Douglas Webb's recommendation not to unbundle and wanted to send the matter back for review. We discussed the issue with Treasury officials and officials in the Prime Minister's department and got the feeling from Treasury that they believed the right thing to do was to support the Commission. However, it was very hard to read where the Prime Minister's department had landed. I widely canvassed many cabinet ministers on the topic. I believed that Paul Swain himself supported his officials' view that the matter should be sent back for review but it went to Cabinet, and after some debate the government adopted the Commerce Commission's recommendation. At no stage did the government respond to my letter to Paul Swain about the broadband target, directly or indirectly.

We put in place marketing programmes to try to lift our broadband take-up rate so that we could achieve the 250,000 household target. Many people in the company were uncomfortable with what seemed like such an audacious target given our current broadband customer base, and felt that we would be strongly criticised if we did not reach it. On the other hand, many saw it as a challenge and found it motivating and invigorating. As at January 2004 we had achieved 85 per cent broadband coverage of New Zealand, and through our deal with BCL had a goal of 95 per cent by January 2005.

Throughout this period when the government was deliberating and deciding what to do, we could not believe some of the commentary from financial analysts: 'Regulator in your pocket — upgrade to buy', screamed one report.[18] Did these people think that officials, regulators and ministers didn't read this stuff, only offshore investors?

As part of the intense lobbying by all sides, in early February 2004, TelstraClear, Slingshot and ihug got going on the 'Call For Change' campaign in favour of greater regulation of Telecom. I thought that TelstraClear's regulatory doublespeak was breathtaking, as at the same time its parent company Telstra, across the ditch in Australia, dropped its retail broadband prices below the wholesale levels it charged its competitors, such as AAPT. The Australian media talked about the oestrogen-charged world of New Zealand telcos and called Rosemary Howard 'Thelma' to my 'Louise'. Indeed, between Rosemary, myself and Annette Presley, the co-owner and figurehead for Call Plus/Slingshot, I guess it was pretty oestrogen heavy! As part of TelstraClear's lobbying, Rosemary said that if the government had adopted local-loop unbundling Telstra would have spent hundreds of millions of dollars extending its existing broadband network in New Zealand. (A few years later the government did implement unbundling, and have we seen hundreds of millions of dollars of extra investment from Telstra in New Zealand? Of course not.)

I think ultimately the government decided that if they'd sent the Commerce Commission's recommendation back for review there would have been further delay, and that some ministers were concerned to be seen to be supporting the Commission. After all, it had been investigating the subject rigorously for the previous 12 months. Indeed, one commentator who endorsed the government's decision asked why it would have a regulator to conduct reviews if it was going to ignore its recommendations, and that to have rejected Douglas's recommendation would have undermined the standing of the Commerce Commission in future regulatory decisions.

There was much to-do some time later about lobbying by Telecom when the letter I'd written to Paul Swain was made public. This rather overlooked the fact that all the telcos had been lobbying the minister at that time, and that there had long been bilateral communication and commitment between the government and Telecom. Indeed, the Kiwi Share had never been enshrined in legislation: it had always been a bilateral agreement between the Crown and Telecom, which we had agreed to update in 2000 to include basic internet access. My letter may have had some effect on the final decision, although I think that the bigger picture was that the government was keen to get momentum on broadband. They had appointed an expert to make a recommendation, and he'd made it. The arguments for and against unbundling by the various submitters were pretty evenly balanced, and they didn't want to send the matter back for another six months' review. It was time to get on with it.

About this same time, along with our partner BCL, we picked up several regions as part of the government's regional broadband project Probe. The focus of Probe was delivering broadband access to all of the country's 2700 schools, and thus their local communities, by the second quarter of 2005. Ultimately Telecom was awarded 11 out of 14 of the regions, with smaller players winning the other three. (TelstraClear didn't bid for any of the regions.) At the time we were pleased about this, but it probably contributed to the perspective that there wasn't enough competition in the broadband market.

Early in 2004 I decided it was time to do something Telecom hadn't done for a long time: stage a roadshow for retail investors around New Zealand. We spent a lot of time talking to fund managers and potential new institutional investors overseas, and I had long been of the view that it was a real problem that only 25 per cent of Telecom was owned by New Zealanders. I felt there weren't enough New Zealanders with a stake in the company's strong financial performance compared to the situation with the more broad-based sale of tranches of Telstra stock in Australia. So I hopped in a car with Mark Flesher, head of

Above: My sister Marion's christening, with me on the right, Wellington, 1965 — I think the fashions and hairstyles of the time sported by my mother and her two sisters here look very cool now!

Below: My parents, Marion and John, my mother's mother Betty Clay and we four girls, at a family Christmas party at Kodak where my grandmother worked, 1967.

Above: Me (left) with my sisters Angela and Marion on a family holiday in Christchurch, 1968.
Below: Me in the standard format school photo, age 9, 1971.

Above: Me, age 11 (top right); Yvonne, age 10 (top left); Angela, age 9 (front left), and Marion (named after our mother), age 7, 1973.
Below: John Savage and me at home, Point Howard, Wellington, 1988.

Above: Me when I was general manager – marketing, Telecom in 1995. I loved this photo and used it long after it was decent in terms of length of time elapsed since the shot had been taken!
Below: John and me at a Telecom function in 1995.

New Zealand Herald

Above: At the press conference announcing my appointment as CEO of Telecom, August 1999 — me, retiring chairman Peter Shirtcliffe and incoming chairman and former CEO, Roderick Deane.

Below: Roderick Deane and me with Bill Gates in Seattle, October 1999.

Telecom NZ Ltd

Above left: Pride's a very relaxed horse and pretty much 'bomb proof' — he didn't even mind standing still to have his photo taken! 2000.

Above right: Mickey was a wonderful character — very affectionate and quite striking and John took many photos of him. Since then, I seem to have specialised in cats with disabilities — Urchin, one of the two cats I have now, is blind and my previous cat Portia was deaf. 2000.

Right: Cover of *Grace*, April 2000.

Below: Ngati Whatua kaumatua Danny Tumahai and me at the dawn launch of the Southern Cross cable on Takapuna Beach, Auckland, November 2000.

Above: This cartoon featured in *NBR*'s Shoeshine column, which speculated that Telecom had bought into INL to make it more difficult for News Corporation to buy more of INL. May 26, 2000.

Below: This cartoon also featured in the Shoeshine column. When Telstra bought Saturn in February 2000, Telecom shares lost 46 cents in one morning. By November 2001 Telstra had also bought Clear and this column speculated that TelstraClear would struggle to compete with Telecom. November 16, 2001.

The Dominion

Telecom NZ Ltd

Above left: The wall-to-wall coverage of my appointment as CEO of Telecom meant I went from having no public profile to a high one, literally overnight. August 13, 1999.
Above right: Me presenting at the Telecom Network Centre, 2003.
Below: Helen Clark and me at an arts event, 2001.

Telecom NZ Ltd

investor relations, and John Goulter, head of communications, and we drove from north to south telling the Telecom story.

It was great fun. I've always loved getting out and about around New Zealand. Every part of the country has its own charm, from the beautiful beaches of the North Island to the majestic mountains of the South. And it reminded me again that people who live in different parts of New Zealand do see things differently. The roadshow itself, however, was mainly preaching to the converted, i.e. people who already had shares in the company. It didn't make a material difference to getting more local investment in the company.

I also had many interactions with ministers during those months, either formally or informally, some due to being on the government's Growth and Innovation Advisory Board, some due to functions I hosted or attended, and some due to Telecom specifically requesting meetings. There were plenty of opportunities for ministers to give me any direct messages had they so desired.

It was in March 2004 that I first met John Key, then National Party communications spokesperson. I was immediately struck by his grasp of the issues, his appreciation of where a normal, non-technical person would come from, and his easy and relaxed manner — all hallmarks which would play out on the national stage in New Zealand over the following few years.

Also in March I made a quick trip to Hong Kong to present at a huge Credit Suisse First Boston investor conference. Those conferences were always hard work — sitting in a small conference room all day meeting different groups of investors, one after another, but my message that we would be focused on managing the business as it was, rather than aggressively trying to grow, was well received.

An area where we did see potential to both grow and to support our customers better was the IT market. In June 2004 we bought the IT integration company Gen-i and, in July, Computerland. Pip Greenwood, a partner at law firm Russell McVeagh and part of the team acting for us on the purchase, called me late on the night of the negotiations to say she thought Gen-i was closer to doing a deal with another party than to doing one with us. I immediately instructed the Telecom team to finalise the transaction as soon as possible and we completed the deal. We combined the businesses with the existing Telecom IT division (Telecom Advanced Solutions) under the Gen-i name.

At the time, the team in Telecom Advanced Solutions assumed that when we'd bought Gen-i and Computerland we would absorb them and go forward under the Telecom brand name. However, I believed it would be much more powerful to retain the Gen-i brand. I felt some people might struggle to give their telecommunications and IT business to one organisation, and I thought a separate brand would aid the perception of Telecom's reach spreading into IT, and also make that team feel like they were pursuing a new frontier.

Over time this came to be seen as the right call. It was a tricky balance though, because Telecom New Zealand wasn't the only telco that believed the future lay in the IT space. Other telcos around the world had tried and largely failed to make that shift, with some very spectacular failures, such as the AT&T–BT Concert alliance.

It is hard to merge the culture of a telco sales force with an IT services company. For customers, telecommunications is all about total reliability, while IT is all about flexibility. Customers expect a telecommunications company running IT services to have that same high degree of reliability but still be able to customise — quite a hard balance to achieve. It was quite a painful birth, but one aided by the committed leadership of both Mark Ratcliffe as chief information officer and chief operating officer Simon Moutter, who together role-modelled the need to have a culture shift that brought together the best of both the telco sales perspective and the IT services perspective.

Industry commentators were sceptical when we bought Gen-i and Computerland, but by 2006 we were the number one IT player in New Zealand as measured by the IDC Asia Pacific IT Services Tracker survey, a position that has been maintained since. Interestingly, it was never much commented upon that Telecom went on to secure some of the biggest customer wins in New Zealand in the IT space.

During this period we were running a process of appointing two more directors for the Telecom board, both of whom could potentially be chairman when Roderick Deane decided to finish. I was with a colleague early in 2004 when they were called by Wayne Boyd about matters to do with Auckland International Airport, of which he was chair. I'd never met Wayne, so I checked with Mark Verbiest, Telecom's group general counsel, who knew him and regarded him highly. At that stage he wasn't on the list of names that the recruiter had prepared for the board so I asked that he be added to the list. He made the shortlist, became a director and the rest, as they say, is history. When Roderick left Telecom in June 2006, Wayne became chairman, after having been on the board for the previous couple of years. A lawyer by training, Wayne had a background in both law and merchant banking and was a professional company director. At the time he became chairman of Telecom he was also chairman of Meridian Energy, Freightways and Auckland International Airport.

Given the high, and rising, proportion of Australian investors in Telecom, we'd started doing at least one results announcement a year in Sydney. Having a stronger presence in Australia, positive momentum, and the sheer novelty of a female CEO meant that Telecom got lots of coverage in the Australian media, largely positive. With the exception of Gail Kelly, then chief executive of St George Bank, hardly any Australian women headed up large publicly listed companies, but interestingly the media, especially the *Australian Financial Review*, often covered matters to do with corporate women. I received a fair amount of coverage, overwhelmingly positive, and was often asked to speak to businesswomen's groups in Australia. Over the years I was also a very regular speaker at Trans-Tasman Business Circle lunches in Sydney and Melbourne.

We presented our results for the quarter to March in Australia in May 2004, and one analyst from Macquarie's reported that revenue performance was so good it was hard to believe. Acquisitions were by now clearly on the back burner. I believe that grand acquisitions often lead to grand write-downs and said so. The quarterly result of a 17.8 per cent increase in tax-paid profits to $232 million was better than most analysts had predicted, and there's no doubt at that point that we were riding a real high. Being a CEO is a stimulating, interesting job and there's no greater feeling than when your company is going well.

Also in May 2004 I attended the first trans-Tasman Leadership Forum at Government House in Wellington. A high-powered group of Australian and New Zealand businesspeople and politicians gathered to generate a shared agenda to both countries' mutual benefit. This first forum made only modest steps towards this, although some progress has been made since.

On a lighter note, in July 2004 I hosted Helen Clark at the opening of the Telecom-sponsored International Film Festival in Auckland. The film was *The Motorcycle Diaries*, the story of a trip by Che Guevara and Alberto Granado through Latin America in 1952. A little piece in the *Herald*[19] noted that it would be hard to imagine a person less likely to flirt with political revolutionary chic than me, which made me laugh because it was probably true.

...but losing the war

I can remember going for a walk around Oriental Bay, Wellington, with Philip King, general manager – corporate affairs, in May 2004, shortly after the government's decision came out and we were seen to have 'won' the unbundling debate. Philip said to me, 'You know, TG [what most of my team called me], this won't be the end of it. It'll come around again.' I said, 'Mmm, I'm not sure. I don't think the desire to regulate telecommunications will go away but I think it will come back in a different form.' Neither of us was to know that we were both right. The unbundling issue did come back, in relatively short order and with another, much worse, form of intervention from an incumbent telco's perspective — operational separation.

In hindsight, we won the battle but lost the war. Winning the unbundling debate and being awarded so many Probe regions only served to harden the perception that there was little real choice in the market. Indeed, inside observers commented to me later that many in the Labour Cabinet the day the decision was made on unbundling saw it as unfinished business to be dealt with again later.

However, the media stories in both Australia ('Telecom New Zealand reaps rewards of staying the course') and New Zealand ('Telecom basks in rosy glow'[20]) were pretty positive, and by August our share price had broken through $6. Commentators were saying that we looked to have both TelstraClear and the regulators where we wanted them ('Kiwi telco is pick of the bunch'[21]). Our full-year profit announced in August of that year was $754 million, a 6.3 per cent rise in earnings on the previous year, and our shares hit a three-year high of $6.27.

Apparently I was effervescent in announcing the full-year result and all the photos show me happy and smiling. It was relief! To the 99.9 per cent of the population who have never been in that situation, the pressure of reporting on your performance to the market every 12 weeks is gruelling, so it's always good to have some positive news to share.

If it seems like I'm going from talking about one profit result to the next, that's because that's how it often felt. Over time we got faster and faster at compiling the results for each quarter and producing them for the market. Nevertheless, around the time of presenting the results or very soon after, the next month's financials would roll in, which we would then analyse. We would then conduct performance reviews with each division, so it felt like we were never off the treadmill. I was always aware of what the analysts' expectations were, and every good quarter meant the bar got raised even higher.

Importantly, our marketing efforts in mobile were starting to pay off and we started to capture a greater share of new mobile business growth. We announced that we would be upgrading our 027 network through a third-generation technology known as EVDO (1xRTT) later in 2004. The subsequent Telecom 3G advertising campaign won three Effies at the New Zealand Advertising and Communication Awards, including the grand award for Advertiser of the Year in 2005. I loved that campaign and felt quite moved when we first presented it to customers. It was an exciting time leading the first company to launch a 3G mobile network in New Zealand.

Another very pleasant event came in June 2004, when Simon Moutter and I hosted a dinner for people who'd worked for Telecom or its predecessors for 40 years or more. I had started this tradition a few years into my time as CEO and did it every year. There were usually somewhere between 30 and 50 people who were marking their 40-year anniversaries each year, and it was always a joy to mix with them and to celebrate past, present and future at the company.

I felt on a high with the way things were going for the business, but after nearly five years as CEO, working at a gruelling pace in a relentless environment, I started to get some physical manifestations of stress. As well as my experience of TMJ, earlier on in my career I had also suffered from back problems which were often exacerbated in times of stress. Fortunately they had been dealt with easily by an osteopath. This time the stress manifested itself in the form of skin irritations, so I started seeing an iridologist and naturopath. She told me I was dehydrated, not drinking enough water and consuming too much sugar. I tried hard to start drinking more water but I didn't really make any effort on the sugar front. I've always had a very sweet tooth and while I'm very disciplined about most things in life, including exercise, I'm very undisciplined about eating.

I enjoy physical activity, and since my brush with TMJ and the pain of that in my mid-twenties, swimming every day had become non-negotiable for me. When I travelled I cared much more about the size of the swimming pool at the hotel than I did about the size of the room! I have swum first thing every morning wherever I am in the world. There would have only been a few days in the last 22 years when I've missed a swim: a very few times when I've been too sick to physically get out of bed, the period after I broke my arm in a fall from my horse and couldn't go into the water, and occasionally when I've been overseas in a location more than an hour's drive away from a swimming pool.

To help keep myself in good shape, for many years I have also had a massage most weeks, and while I was CEO most months I would have a session with a gifted healer, Meryl Yvonne. It's hard to describe what she did — I think of it as rebalancing my energies and restoring them whenever they were depleted.

I had another scare that winter too. I've always loved Queenstown and this year I spent Queen's Birthday Weekend there with my sister Angela. I've never been a great driver, and coming down Coronet Peak in a rental four-wheel-drive I found I was unable to stop it sliding on the icy road. I was terrified as we slid towards the edge of a cliff without any barriers. I screamed at my sister to get out as I turned the wheel into the side of the hill.

Angela managed to scramble out, though she only narrowly avoided going under the wheels, and I managed to scramble out too, into the ditch. The car continued to slide a further 50 metres down the icy mountain road and ended up nose-down in the ditch on the mountain side rather than going off the cliff. I was so shaken I could hardly speak. One minute we were sailing down the mountain — slightly too fast, obviously — and the next minute I thought my beloved sister and I were going to perish! We flagged down some skifield workers who were coming down the mountain to help get the car out of the ditch and drive it and us down the hill. As soon as we got to the bottom, my sister had the presence of mind to instruct me to immediately start driving again — she thought I would lose my nerve entirely if I didn't 'get back on the horse'. It was the last thing I felt like doing but it was probably a good call on her part — and, of course, a supreme act of confidence given I'd just nearly driven both of us off a cliff!

On a more positive note, by this time I'd also got into owning race horses. My friend Cindy Mitchener had hooked me up with her mate Mark Todd (voted Equestrian of the Twentieth Century by the International Equestrian Federation) when he came back to live in New Zealand and I invested in several syndicates with horses that he'd picked out. One in particular was a horse named Bramble Rose, a name John had discovered by putting my name into a website that generated my 'hobbit name'! Bramble Rose was owned in a syndicate which, among others, included Mark himself and broadcaster Paul

Holmes. She was New Zealand Filly of the Year in 2002–2003 and was very successful on the racetrack, winning the New Zealand Oaks in 2003 and finishing third in the AJC Oaks at Randwick in Sydney. Unfortunately she suffered an injury in that race and was never the same again. Eventually we sold her to a breeder in Australia who put her to the top sire of the year in Australia, Redoubt's Choice, and she got into foal straight away.

On the back of this early success I bought more racehorses, but I was soon to discover that owning racehorses is a bit like having a venture capital portfolio. Only one in 10 is fantastic, two will be okay and the rest will be duds. It was my misfortune to discover that my first one was the star, and although I've owned several racehorses since I've never reached the giddy heights of regularly winning Group One races as I did in my first season as a racehorse owner.

By the time of the Telecom AGM in October 2004, broadband was available to 93 per cent of all customers and we were gaining a new broadband customer every seven minutes. We were doing as many broadband sales in a weekend as it had taken a month to do just a year previously, and the number of residential customers rose 65 per cent year on year to over 120,000. But as Simon Moutter noted at the Telecom quarterly profit result, broadband was not going to be cashflow positive within a two-year timeframe, let alone start making profits. We needed to spend capital to drive growth, so we increased our full-year capital expenditure forecast to $700 million.

As promised, in November we launched our 3G mobile phone network in Auckland, Wellington, Christchurch and holiday spots. We had beaten Vodafone to the punch, as they weren't due to launch their 3G network until some time in the first half of 2005. At the same time we launched the network, the Commerce Commission issued a draft determination proposing to regulate mobile termination prices — the prices telcos charge each other for calls between networks. This was the first time the Commission had moved to regulate mobile and we had some concerns about the potential issues around this.

However, the launch of 3G proved a significant step for the mass take-up of personal digital assistants (PDAs) and high-speed data cards for laptops.

In the six months to December 2004, mobile revenue growth was 15.8 per cent per annum, but most importantly and satisfyingly, for the three months to December we added a further 96,000 mobile connections, outstripping Vodafone's growth for the same period of 74,000. It was the first time in several years that Telecom had added a lot more customers than Vodafone.

Being on CDMA technology (using EVDO) had allowed us to get to 3G faster then Vodafone, but even though at that time CDMA had 200 million users worldwide and was the standard mobile technology in the United States, GSM, which was the Vodafone standard, had 1.2 billion users worldwide. We were always challenged in terms of choice of handsets because there just weren't as many different CDMA models being made compared to GSM-compatible ones. GSM was in the ascendancy and more handsets and services were being designed for that technology, which had been part of the success of Vodafone in New Zealand. This was particularly a problem for us because on a global basis the quantity of handsets that Telecom New Zealand was ordering was miniscule.

Our team came up with a very innovative partnership with US cellphone giant Sprint, who used a CDMA network, which meant better economies of scale, i.e. the manufacturers were making handsets for a much bigger company. We were able to piggyback on Sprint's supplier deal simply by changing our mobile network slightly so that phones designed for its network were able to work here. It was an innovative approach to dealing to what was a perennial problem with CDMA.

In November we also launched access for competitors to the regulated Bitstream wholesale service, as previously specified by the Telecommunications Commissioner — the first piece of wholesale regulation to come into force. Broadband growth was taking off, with a record number of new residential customers in the three months to September.

All year we had signalled to the market that we needed to invest in both mobile and broadband and that's what we were quietly doing. At that quarter's profit result the costs associated with those investments were beginning to drag on our earnings performance. Still, it had been a very satisfying year.

personal travails

Meanwhile, things still weren't great on the home front, and they were about to get worse. On top of our other issues, John's father was diagnosed with terminal cancer. Pat and Ralph Savage lived at Waihi Beach at the base of the Coromandel Peninsula, where John and I had bought a bach many years previously. John was deeply upset by news of his father's illness and was still struggling to find a way to move forward in his chosen field, having completed his photography qualification through Massey a year earlier. He travelled up to Waihi Beach regularly during this time, never knowing when he might end up going to a funeral.

In August 2004 John had his first public exhibition at a dealer gallery in Sydney, which was a fantastic achievement given the short time that he'd been a photographer, and fortunately I was able to organise my schedule to be at the opening to support him. However, just a couple of months later, in late October 2004, Ralph died quietly at home, three months after his diagnosis. We were both there, along with the rest of John's family, when he died. Pat was exhausted after the months looking after Ralph at home, although she had received wonderful support from a local hospice.

During my two decades with John, I'd spent a lot of time with his family. In fact, I'd been friends with John's sister, Andrea, at university before he and I got together. John's parents had always welcomed me into their family and we'd enjoyed many happy times together, especially at Waihi Beach, where we had spent many summer holidays, John surfing and me pottering about.

Obviously this was a very difficult time for John, but I probably didn't read the signs as well as I should have about what was to come. At some level I must have known something was very wrong, however, because around the end of the year my skin problems got steadily worse and I had to wear heavier and heavier make-up to camouflage them.

In mid-March 2005 I flew straight back from a week in Australia to my friend Pip Greenwood's wedding in Queenstown. It was a gorgeous Central Otago day and a lovely wedding. The speeches made by Pip, her husband David Gibson and her father were all wonderful and I was very happy for her, but I also felt sad inside because at the last minute John hadn't been able to accompany me. Being at such a happy occasion, I couldn't help but reflect on the fact that things were seriously flat between us. There just wasn't the connection there used to be.

John and I went to our place at Waihi Beach for Easter but we were not as settled and content in each other's company as we had always been previously. The following week, on the Tuesday evening, John came home and said he'd decided to leave, and was going to stay with his best friend. In the few days leading up to this we had done something we had never done before, which was to actively fight.

He told me he'd been having an affair. I was devastated. I knew the woman involved, and while she and John were equally culpable, I found myself blaming her. I have thought about my reaction often since. Given my strong feminist views, why was I able to forgive John, who apologised to me in great distress, and with whom I continue to have a strong friendship, while I have never spoken to her since and have no desire to do so? Why did I blame her? Is there some deep biological thing that means when another woman takes your man you forgive him but not her?

Their affair had in fact ended a few weeks prior to our break-up, but John saw it as a big wake-up call that he was not living the life that he wanted. I was deeply upset of course, but I was never angry with him because I'd seen how depressed and miserable he was, how much he was suffering, and what a difficult year he'd been through with the death of his father. I could see that he needed to be in his own space, away from the constant train station that was my life and in a more contemplative environment. While during my first anxious years as CEO John had been a great support for me, over time he became less emotionally present. He was dealing with his own struggle to find his way professionally, and as a very private person he had finally had enough of doing the corporate spouse bit.

The week of our break-up coincided with a two-day board meeting, a strategic retreat. I did my very best to hold it together, but both Roderick Deane and Mark Verbiest realised that something was wrong, although I didn't explain anything to them at that point. I confided in only one or two of my closest women friends.

It only took John and me a couple of conversations to sort things out on a practical level. Fortunately he wanted to leave Wellington, so did not want to live in our apartment. There were no children, just our cat, Mickey, who we both loved. Mickey had never enjoyed being in the apartment and after John left, because I was out all the time, he became very sad. We made the decision to give him to John's mum, and Mickey was great company for Pat for several years until he died. Animals can be the most wonderful companions, giving their owners so much joy. And they have so much to teach us about trust and forgiveness, and about giving people another chance even when they have been hurt! I knew it was the right decision, but from the day John came to take Mickey away it was very hard to be in the apartment by myself with no one else and no animals for the first time in my entire life.

It didn't take us very long to agree what we considered a fair division of our assets. But our experience when we went to talk to lawyers to get a formal separation document drawn up was very revealing.

I went to see a top divorce lawyer in Auckland, who pretty quickly advised me that I was being too generous. After all, we weren't married and didn't have any kids. Meanwhile, John went to a local neighbourhood matrimonial property lawyer in one of the inner Auckland suburbs and got exactly the opposite advice — that he should go for more. We told both lawyers just to proceed on the basis we had already agreed. John's lawyer asked him to sign a document saying that she'd given him advice to the contrary and he was ignoring it!

One or two of my closest friends also thought I was being quite generous, but I simply saw it as fair given the years that John had supported me. I think his support of me in the 22 years we'd been together was without precedent in terms of the support I'd ever seen any other woman receive. I knew John's passion for photography meant that his income-earning potential in the future would be much lower than mine, and I wanted to feel good about how I'd handled matters.

Interestingly, our separation never really featured in the media. When it was commented on a little later, it seemed to be assumed that I had left him — an interesting commentary, perhaps, on the perspective that the person with the most economic power in a relationship is the one who calls the shots?

We remain friends to this day and I continue to value John's insights and advice. Of course we changed our wills, but we've still left things to each other we accumulated during our time together.

After John left, the reality took a while to sink in. Because I had always been away a lot and we were still talking regularly on the phone, it just felt like it was one of those periods where we weren't seeing that much of each other. But gradually it became all too real: me always being by myself in the apartment and waking up alone in what had been our queen-sized bed.

I did a lot of travel in 2005; to London, the United States (twice) and Hong Kong to meet investors, to Sydney and Melbourne to meet investors and customers and to talk to politicians. In particular I found Helen Coonan, who was then Australian Minister of Communications, a superb politician, able to see all sides of at times complex issues.

One of the reasons we needed to spend so much time overseas in 2005 talking to overseas investors was because the Australian government was preparing to sell a stake in Telstra, and we knew many fund managers would potentially sell Telecom New Zealand shares to buy Telstra. As about 75 per cent of Telecom was owned by overseas investors, this was potentially a real risk to us. On the other hand, some members of the financial community, when asked about whether they would switch out of Telecom into Telstra, made comments like, 'Well, we prefer Telecom because it's a better monopoly'!

And of course I continued to travel all around New Zealand — Auckland, Tauranga, Christchurch — meeting customers and talking to staff. I also accompanied the company's top sales people on a trip to Mexico (the first time I'd gone on a reward-and-recognition trip in my time as CEO), travelled to Fiji where my youngest sister Marion was celebrating her fortieth birthday, and took myself off to a health spa in Australia for a few days during the winter. Good friends took me off to Queenstown for a couple of weekends over that winter too.

Although much of this travel was prescheduled, I also think it was the way I chose to deal with what had happened. Some people tend to go inwards and become reflective at times of personal challenge. Partly because I didn't have the option of doing that and partly because of my personality, I chose to keep moving. Indeed, when I told Philip King the night before addressing our top 100 staff at

a leadership day that John and I were separating, his advice to me
was that whatever I did, I mustn't let anyone say it was making any
difference to my performance, on the grounds that it's not a good
thing for a CEO to appear in any way weak or vulnerable. He was
right, of course. In fact, I felt that leadership day was one of my most
powerful, perhaps because I felt more vulnerable than usual but was
determined to hide it.

At a personal level, I had great support from my women friends
during this time, in particular Chris Woodwiss, my assistant who had
become a very close friend, and Margaret Doucas, a longstanding
close friend, who cooked a lot of meals for me during that period.
(John had been the cook in our household.) Nevertheless, whatever
my outward appearance, I felt emotionally drained and mixed
up that entire year and only started to feel like myself again about
Christmastime.

In contrast, 2005 started very well workwise. We were all very upbeat
at the February results presentation — 'brimming with confidence'
was how one analyst described it. Sometimes it is indeed a blessing
that you do not know what life has in store for you just around the
corner! Debt was down, dividends were up, the threat of local loop
unbundling was at bay, broadband connections were on a high
growth curve and mobile was finally holding its own against global
giant Vodafone.

Every quarter that year we outperformed Vodafone. Being the
first to launch 3G and $10 texting were the two main catalysts, and by
December we had rolled out our third-generation mobile broadband
network, T3G, to every main town and city in New Zealand.

Our alliance with US telco giant Sprint had helped considerably
by linking us into Sprint's buying group for mobile handsets, an area
where we had previously been less competitive than Vodafone. But by
then Sol Trujillo had been appointed CEO of Telstra in Australia, and
in November 2005 it was announced that Telstra would shut down its
CDMA network. This was a huge blow for Telecom because Australia

is the most popular roaming destination for New Zealanders. It meant we immediately had to consider a technology switch, even though CDMA was going very well.

Our biggest investment project in 2005 was the billion-dollar plan to replace the existing telephone network with a managed internet protocol (IP) network. The move to such a network would pave the way for Telecom to produce a raft of new, 'intelligent' phone services. Our vision was that the traditional fixed-line phone number, which is really a household phone number, would disappear. All customers would be given the option of having one or more contact numbers which they would be able to allocate to any phone at any time, and over which they would have individual control. Customers would truly be at the heart of the network. We envisaged reducing the number of telephone exchanges from about 600 throughout New Zealand to 20 to 30.

I freely admitted that we did not know how this would translate exactly into products, prices and ultimately profits, but I fervently believed that customers themselves would determine what the new services would look like. This was the same thing I had frequently said about mobile services: it wasn't telco execs who saw how big texting would become, it was customers who seized upon it, first in the consumer market and then as a normal part of doing business.

At this time Telecom was seen as a very well-run company with a confident and highly competent management team. Analysts commented positively on the totally transparent nature of the financial community briefing days we held. While some companies chose to hide behind the complexity of their industries, we were very upfront and honest about the challenges we faced and what we were trying to do about them. I seldom prepared a formal presentation and usually spoke just from notes and from the heart.

In fact, heart was quite a key word for me. It had taken me a long time to get comfortable talking to the financial community, mainly because my style, whether in one-on-one sessions or talking with groups, is to integrate an intellectual, 'head' perspective and an emotional, 'heart' perspective. In the early days I found the financial community the hardest group to do that with because I believed it was only ever all about the numbers for them, but over time I'd come to realise that they were just a bunch of human beings like any other, with a range of talents, personalities and perspectives, and by early 2005 I was very comfortable dealing with them.

Being under a little less pressure results-wise we had the luxury of time to consider matters like staff development. My head of human resources, Trisha McEwan, was passionate about leadership development. Her assessments of the Telecom top 100 leadership team had shown very high performance in terms of IQ, but rather patchier results in terms of EQ or emotional intelligence, so each person in the top 100 was given the option to be part of a personalised leadership development programme. I had been part of many different leadership programmes during my career, but people told me this one added real value to how they saw themselves and helped them to become more well rounded. I think emotional intelligence is vital for leaders because it doesn't matter how strong your ideas are, if you can't interact well with others, your overall effectiveness will be weakened. Business is much more about people than it is about balance sheets. People follow people.

There are a lot of practitioners of dross in the consultancy game, but people who are good at what they do leave an imprint on all those they touch. For me in my time as CEO, the consultant who had the greatest effect was Elan (just the one name!) of Breakthrough International. He was already working in another part of Telecom when I became CEO and was highly regarded. I worked with him as a catalyst to accelerate the bonding process in my top team. We'd go off-site to places like the Martinborough Hotel for a day and a half and work through our belief set, our power to affect outcomes, what we were committed to, and our responsibilities as leaders. I found this to be very effective and long after Simon Moutter and I had left Telecom we concluded it was still the most powerful programme of its type that we'd been involved in or seen in action.

I went to Australia regularly during this period. By February of 2005 we were conducting our investor briefing days in Sydney because the next new investor was much more likely to be an Australian fund manager than a New Zealand one. And in April I went to the second Australia New Zealand Leadership Forum held in Melbourne.

In December 2004, I had had dinner at the Shangri-La Hotel in Sydney with the CEO of SingTel Optus, Paul O'Sullivan, and Trevor Rowe, chairman of investment bank Rothschild Australia. Paul suggested the meeting, to discuss SingTel Optus buying AAPT. He followed up in January with a letter proposing that we jointly explore options, including the creation of a joint venture between Telecom New Zealand's businesses in Australia and SingTel Optus.

At that stage we were not considering selling AAPT, but it seemed worth exploring. We had succeeded in getting the Australian business into a stable position where it was no longer bleeding cash but it was very difficult to make much further headway. Although there was unbundling in Australia, wholesale was not regulated in the way that it was in New Zealand by then, so we were very open to SingTel Optus's approach. It seemed a natural fit, among other reasons because they had no presence in the New Zealand market, so they weren't competing with Telecom. After Paul's overtures to us, we spent a considerable amount of time over the next 10 months looking at every possible permutation of a deal. Marko and I were both surprised when Paul rang Marko in October to say that they had decided not to put anything formal on the table in relation to Telecom's Australian assets.

Had they been genuine, or was that a 10-month tyre-kicking exercise, making it very difficult for Telecom to plan for AAPT's future? I think they were genuine, but then I generally do tend to believe the best of people.

There was certainly plenty on at work to keep me busy. During that year and in 2006, two of New Zealand's largest corporate customers — Westpac and the Ministry of Justice — put their telecommunications up for tender and I was personally quite involved in both bids which, following rigorous processes, we went on to win. Somewhat unusually, in both situations, the key CEO decision-makers were women: Ann Sherry, CEO of Westpac, and Belinda Clark, Secretary of the Ministry of Justice.

Interestingly, as my personal life was going into meltdown, Telecom's share price was riding high, hitting $6.50 in early April 2005. Little did I know that it would never — up till the time of writing— reach those heights again.

The year-end profit for the year to June 2005 was $916 million, including a one-off gain of $86 million from the sale of Telecom's stake in INL. It seems unlikely that Telecom will ever make profits at this level or anything approaching it again.

From time to time I have wondered whether I was even more discombobulated than I realised, and whether I missed some signs in the eight months from April to the end of the year that at another time I might have heeded. Certainly the press about Telecom was all positive in the first quarter of 2005, but by the end of the year it was starting to be laced with a heavier degree of criticism.

In early May I had warned that Telecom's future profits would be hit by our investment in new technologies, and the share price never really recovered from that. Herein lay the nub of the problem. Although we were spending more on capital expenditure every year, mainly to drive broadband growth, it was never enough for those who thought that we should simply be acting as a good corporate citizen and increasing that capital expenditure figure even further.

Our involvement with the New Zealand government continued. From the winter of 2004 I started meeting regularly with David Cunliffe, who had been the Associate Minister of Communications since May 2003 and became the Minister of Communications in December 2004. I had several meetings with him during May and June 2005. During this period, conversation was dominated not by broadband matters but by mobile termination.

The Telecommunications Commission had recommended that

mobile termination be a regulated service for mobile calls on second-generation technology and mobile calls if they were on Telecom's third-generation network but not on Vodafone's third-generation network. This was seen as nonsensical by the wider industry (and probably the minister and officials) and we worked to make a commercial offer that included all 2G and 3G calls and put that in front of the minister. We then released this publicly as part of a process of it being returned to the Commission for reconsideration. (Vodafone objected to their offer being released.)

During this period I attended several social events with David Cunliffe and we had several telephone calls in addition to our face-to-face meetings. He was at pains to tell me that he felt Telecom was dealing with the government and regulatory matters in a highly professional way.

In terms of broadband, we had never heard back from the minister's office (at that time Paul Swain) when we wrote setting out our commitment to a goal of 250,000 households with broadband by the end of 2005 and our expectation that a third of the growth in broadband would come from the wholesale market, i.e. that Telecom would be wholesaling broadband to other telcos such as TelstraClear, who would then retail it to customers. However, some months later Telecommunications Commissioner Douglas Webb wrote to us to say that he would be monitoring the targets of 250,000 households and a third of the total at wholesale, i.e. 83,000. We wrote back to him pointing out that this was not what we had said: we had said a third of the *growth*, not a third of the total. (This letter is in the public domain and what we said is a matter of public record.) He wrote back and said too bad, this is what the ministry has asked me to monitor.

By the winter of 2005 it was clear that we were going to make the target we had set for ourselves of 250,000 broadband customers with two batsmen to spare! But by this time key MPs were already in election mode and David Cunliffe's rhetoric around telecommunications had started to harden. He started to emphasise the importance of the 83,000 wholesale number publicly, although privately he continued to say to me 'a miss is not the same as a mile'. I sent him regular written updates of what we were doing to support our wholesale customers in driving broadband uptake, and to explain that 50 per cent of dial-up customers were our customers, 25 per cent were TelstraClear's and 25 per cent were with other, smaller ISPs. Not only was TelstraClear not driving broadband, it also now had a perverse incentive *not* to do so, given they could expect a better regulatory outcome if they didn't! In response to one of my updates David responded that the government would take action if Telecom didn't meet the broadband and wholesale targets — which, based on what we had committed to, we did.

Clearly we had influence over the total number of broadband customers and continued to drive broadband growth through offers like free connection and installation and dropping the price of entry-level packages to encourage people to migrate from dial-up. We had a clear hierarchy of priorities: the first step was to get broadband reach out as far as we possibly could (that had been the focus in 2004), then to convert the still hundreds of thousands of dial-up customers onto broadband, which was our focus in 2005. The focus of 2006 was going to be on driving sales growth onto higher-speed packages.

In late June, Douglas Webb made a presentation which was critical of our approach to wholesale. He said he thought we were taking a too narrow, commercial approach. Following that we started working on a 'wholesale charter', focused on voluntarily offering service equivalence, i.e. a completely level playing field between Telecom Retail and Telecom's wholesale customers, who were Telecom Retail's competitors (the other telcos and internet service providers).

In early September I flew with the board to Europe to meet with Alcatel, our supplier partner in the fixed-line business in the transition to a managed IP network, France Telecom, 3 Italy and Telecom Italia.

On September 10, while I was waiting in transit at Frankfurt airport, David Cunliffe called me to run through Labour's telecommunications policy. This was the second of two conversations I had with him while I was in Europe. I took careful notes of that call and what David said would be the Labour Party's approach to telecommunications, should they be returned to power. He covered the background, saying how ultra-light-handed legislation had stifled competition, recounting how in 2001 Labour had brought telecommunications policy into line internationally by setting up the Telecommunications Commissioner and sorting out interconnection and number portability issues.

In 2004 the government had accepted the recommendation of the Commerce Commission and gone for wholesaling rather than unbundling, and the challenge now was to build on that platform. He said the goal was to bring the benefits of internet and communications technology (ICT) to all and that Labour's priorities were to:

- implement the digital strategy, the components of which were to
    - unlock digital content
    - build capability in the sector
    - grow broadband, and
    - promote demand
- complete an implementation review of the 2001 Telecommunications Act no later than the end of 2006
- address any remaining issues around wholesale
- consider broadband uptake targets
- implement a Telecommunications Complaint Resolution Service
- conduct municipal fibre pilots (i.e. local body fibre networks)
- sort out some spectrum space for non-commercial usage
- implement changes to ICT procurement and procedures in the government sector, and
- work on the government shared network (GSN), linking various government agencies with a secure, high-speed IT & T network.

Did any of that sound like the then Minister of Communications spelling out to the CEO of Telecom in a transparent, straightforward way what

Labour expected to see from Telecom should they regain the Treasury benches? Dear reader, I'll leave you to make up your own mind.

Early one weekday morning, a couple of days after returning from that board trip to Europe, I was hit by a car on a pedestrian crossing outside the swimming pool on the way back to my apartment. It had stopped just short of the crossing, but was shunted into me by a van behind it travelling at high speed. The point of impact was my right hip. I went up over the car's bonnet and landed in the middle of a wet, cold road, on my right side. It all happened so fast, in just a split second.

I knew as soon as I landed on the road, winded and severely shaken, that I hadn't broken anything, just as I had known a few years earlier when I'd been thrown from my horse that I had badly broken my right wrist. Staff from the pool immediately rushed out with oxygen, which they administered to me until an ambulance arrived.

I'd only been in hospital for a few minutes when Mark Verbiest walked in. I thought he'd come to visit me and couldn't understand how he'd heard about the accident so quickly — only to find out that his wife had driven him there as he had been suffering all night with a painful kidney stone. We had a good giggle about that much later.

However, I was almost immediately visited by my wonderful assistant Chris Woodwiss, who asked what underwear I was wearing. I said none: I had just taken off my wet togs, put on my tracksuit and was going back home to get changed to go to work. So it's true, it is those times when you're wearing daggy clothes and no underwear that you have an accident!

Even though it was just two days before the election, Helen Clark called that day to express her concern about the accident. David Cunliffe also called me. I took the day off work, feeling very shaky, but was back at work the next day and made it to my father's seventieth birthday celebrations in Ohope on the Saturday.

I was very bruised all down my right arm and right leg and needed several sessions with my osteopath to sort my body out, but I felt very fortunate that the consequences hadn't been more severe.

Nevertheless, a few years on I do notice now that I am a lot stiffer on my right side than my left, and on top of my daily swimming I need a combination of massage, yoga and other body work to avoid pain in my right hip, which I attribute to a combination of being hit by the car and a couple of earlier falls from my horse, every time onto my right side.

Following Labour's re-election in September we had update meetings with Michael Cullen, Trevor Mallard, Steve Maharey and Jim Anderton, some of the other ministers whose portfolios were impacted by broadband. I had a good relationship with these ministers: I found Jim Anderton practical and action-oriented, I enjoyed Michael Cullen's wit and intelligence, and I got on well with Trevor Mallard. I found him upfront and straight-talking and while I might not always have agreed with him, I always knew where I stood.

At none of these meetings did any of these ministers indicate that anything had fundamentally shifted in their perspective of us or in the telecommunications policy area. We understood that we would need to have a more proactive approach to wholesale, which stemmed from Douglas Webb's prior challenge, and we'd been working for some time on developing the wholesale charter embracing the principles of service equivalence and levelling the playing field between us and our competitors.

Of course, it is entirely possible that in September 2005 the government hadn't yet decided to introduce much heavier-handed telco regulation, which had an immediate and dramatic effect on reducing Telecom's market value. As was revealed later on, this move was intended to be a centrepiece of the May 2006 budget, so at the latest it must have been decided on by early 2006.

In any event, the popular characterisation of events — that Telecom had repeatedly been warned by the government that it must do more to promote broadband and open up its network to competition but had ignored it, thus forcing the government to take action — is not how it was. Either the minister in particular and perhaps others in the Cabinet had decided on a certain course of action between September and December 2005 and chose not to reveal it until later, or they had not decided by then and the policy came together quickly in early 2006 — either way, there was no long, drawn-out period of the government, through either ministers or officials, communicating an expectation of the company that was not taken on board.

Interestingly, between September and December 2005 I had more than my usual number of conversations with Helen Clark. As well as calling me the day of my accident, she called me to discuss who would be the right person to chair the trans-Tasman Leadership Forum from New Zealand's side. She called me to discuss the successful World Cup bid, and we had a Christmas lunch together, with Ann Sherry and a few other CEOs, at Ann's house in December. At no stage in any of these conversations did Helen directly or indirectly touch on telecommunications policy.

In November we presented the wholesale charter to Douglas Webb, then Bruce Parkes, my head of regulatory affairs, and I presented this personally to David Cunliffe and his key officials. I sent David a letter, shared with the board, which addressed discrepancies between what he had said privately to me and what he had said publicly regarding the government's intention to intervene further in telecommunications' policy settings, and suggested we have dinner to discuss how Telecom could work with the government. This we did on November 9, together with Bruce and David's political advisor from his office. It was a perfectly pleasant dinner at which David told me that of course he'd made certain public statements as Labour spokesperson on telecommunications, but now that he was minister it was an entirely different situation! Following the dinner he sent me a card saying that he looked forward to working constructively with Telecom.

Throughout this whole period in late 2005, my conversations with David Cunliffe were dominated by the way Telecom and the government could work together, with me encouraging him to set a new, high, overall broadband target, of which we would sign up for a significant proportion.

During late 2005 the whole environment was clearly worsening from our perspective, with more and more regulation on the cards and increasingly negative media. We discussed this at every board meeting. At no stage was an alternative way of managing the challenges proposed (except occasionally Roderick would push for a more 'hard-nosed' approach). This was not surprising. Our approach had worked extremely well for six years, since the Fletcher Inquiry had first called for a much tougher regulatory regime (including unbundling and cost-based wholesale).

By November the media was basically running the line that we would be dealt to severely by the government should we miss our wholesale broadband target. We decided to point out that our letter to the minister had talked about a third of the *growth*, not a third of the total. This was met with hostility in some quarters of the media, and I noticed the negativity level towards Telecom seemed to have shifted up a gear. The media tended to omit mentioning that we were well ahead of the 250,000 household target, which we actually achieved in October 2005, and focused instead on the wholesale number, or simply ignored both and focused on New Zealand's ranking of 22nd out of 30 OECD countries for broadband performance. We tried to point out that this was a similar ranking to New Zealand's GDP per capita performance and that there was probably a relationship between the two figures, but that didn't fit the narrative of the day so it was ignored.

Every month I pored over customer research, and in this period I commissioned research on how customers felt about broadband — not the normal product research about features and packages and prices, which we regularly did, but more how people felt about it as an *issue*. Insight Research told us that of all the issues they had ever polled, broadband was among the least significant. In other words, it just didn't rate highly as a public concern, although it was clear most people did support unbundling. And indeed we were still winning customer awards. In 2005 Xtra won multiple *PC World* Readers' Choice Awards — for best ISP, best broadband internet service, and best service and support for an ISP (for the fifth year running).

From a customer perspective, most importantly, we knew that business broadband prices needed to come down, but for months the Telecommunications Commissioner had been deliberating on the TelstraClear application for UBS (Bitstream wholesale service) which set the wholesale rate. Many of our marketing initiatives had already been investigated by the Commerce Commission and we thought there was a very high risk, that if we dropped retail prices without having the appropriate wholesale price in place, we would open ourselves up to an investigation around having acted anti-competitively (i.e that we had reduced the retail price to customers but were not fairly allowing our competitors to compete with us because we had not dropped the wholesale price to them). The commissioner's determination came out late December, just before Christmas, which freed us up to move on lowering the retail prices.

But before this happened, in November David Cunliffe announced he would be doing a telecommunications 'stocktake', with an unspecified process and a mid-2006 timeframe. It seems almost unbelievable that the country's biggest publicly listed company and one of its most important industries should be subject to an unspecified review process that had no stated goals, no set of parameters and no draft determination that participants in the industry could comment on, and that something with such huge ramifications for the capital markets should have been treated in such a cavalier fashion, but that is exactly what happened. No regulatory body like the Commerce Commission or Securities Commission would ever be permitted to act in this way. We made it clear we were very concerned about the lack of due process, but no one was interested.

Prior to Christmas we had lunches with Geoff Dangerfield, head of the Ministry of Economic Development, and his senior official David Smol; Maarten Wevers, head of the Prime Minister's department, and other officials from the PM's department. At no stage did we get any indication that sentiment towards Telecom had shifted.

The most damaging thing that happened in this period was a major newspaper playing up my letter to Paul Swain from the previous year, citing it as an example of big business having undue influence over the government and conveniently omitting the fact that we were writing in support of the Commerce Commission's determination. I believe the publication of that letter caused the government to perceive being seen to be too close to Telecom as a political vulnerability.

In November, Helen Clark returned from a visit to Korea and was reported to have said that she felt like a country cousin in relation to the broadband presentations she saw there.[22] In comparison to New Zealand, Korea has 60 million people, with about half living in high-density apartments, and the Korean government had at that point already spent around US$600 million on driving broadband.

I felt that there was no preparedness — by the government, by commentators, by the general public — to face the reality of the poor economics of broadband in a low-population-density country like New Zealand. Suddenly it had become like water — everyone's birthright to have as much as they wanted when they wanted, preferably with someone else paying.

Chapter fourteen

clouds gather

Despite these growing clouds, by the end of the year I was starting to feel more like myself again. I went to Queenstown in January with my sister Angela, but while we were having a nice walk along the Arrow River, my holiday came to an abrupt end. Marko Bogoievski called me to say that the financial results for Australia were not good. It was back to the office to deal with the fallout.

By that time the new Telstra CEO, Sol Trujillo, had aggressively driven up prices for Telstra's wholesale customers such as AAPT. Although at that stage unbundling was regulated in Australia, wholesale was a less regulated regime than in New Zealand.

We immediately called a special board meeting. After doing all the appropriate analysis we brought the information to the board and decided we needed to write down the value of the Australian business, which we announced to the market immediately, on January 20.

Despite the poor Australian result, Simon Moutter, Marko and

I were in quite an upbeat mood when we announced the group financial results on February 2. The mobile business was a stand-out performer. We'd added a further 135,000 mobile connections in the three months to the end of 2005 — twice the number of Vodafone — taking Telecom's market share to just over 47 per cent. Also on the plus side, we announced that we had finished the year with 279,000 residential broadband customers — well ahead of the 250,000 target we'd set ourselves — and of those, 63,500 were wholesale customers, up from 7000 at the same time the previous year, thereby achieving wholesale customers representing a third of the growth in broadband connections that we had actually estimated. We had done everything we could to meet the 83,000 'target'* for wholesale customers but without TelstraClear, the second biggest player in the market, driving broadband, it was nigh on impossible. We had finally been able to do a deal with TelstraClear only after the Commission made its determination in December.

The day before our February profit result, Helen Clark called me as part of an ongoing conversation we were having about the economy in general — whether it really was slowing down. The day after the announcement, the *National Business Review* published a series of stories, leading with the front page, essentially saying that low broadband uptake was a handbrake on the economy and that it was Telecom's fault: 'Telecom Handbrake Stalls the Nation'.[23] It also alleged that Telecom had exerted undue influence on the government in 2004 to avoid unbundling. That day, John Goulter, my head of communications, and I had a lunch with Christopher Niesche, then the business editor of the *New Zealand Herald*, at which he expressed the opinion that the *NBR* story was merely a bunch of assertions. However, it soon became obvious that the *Herald* was planning its own story on broadband the next day[24] and he probably felt that he'd

---

As outlined earlier, this was not the number we had estimated to the government, although it might have been what they understood. Certainly there was no process of checking with us as they never responded to our letter.

been scooped. Following publication of these two stories, Helen no longer returned my calls.

We had already determined a new series of broadband offerings from April 1, which we were going to announce on March 1 as we needed to give our competitors a month's notice. I decided we should announce immediately that from April 1 we would be introducing speed upgrades for residential broadband customers, bringing down prices to business customers and introducing a dollar-a-day broadband. A political source let me know that the government's reaction to this was not to be pleased that we were getting on with it, albeit belatedly from their perspective, but rather to be annoyed that we were beating them to the punch. A couple of days later the Prime Minister said in her opening statement to Parliament for the year that initiatives were needed to get faster internet access at more competitive prices. It became clear to me later that at that point they seemed to have determined there was a political upside in being seen to have a go at Telecom.

The share price rose 16 cents to $5.82 after the result was announced, because we had delivered better than expected growth in New Zealand operating earnings.

By the Friday night of that week I felt shattered. I went to see John, who was by then living in Auckland, before taking myself off to Waihi Beach for the weekend. This was the first time I had seen John at his new place, and it was weird and very unsettling to walk in and see his books, his art, his photography — so many things that had adorned our shared home for more than 20 years. It certainly didn't help how I felt.

Worrying about increased regulation and bringing forward the launch of the new broadband plans weren't the only issues on our plate. Earnings growth, which was always the board's key focus (as indeed the shareholders would expect it to be), had stalled. The March strategy day meeting with the board had brought to a head a tension that had been simmering for a little while. Management believed that the value of the company was best preserved and enhanced by focusing on investment in mobile, broadband and IT, and driving a new business model to take out costs. Broadly speaking, the board agreed with that but they also wanted management to more vigorously explore new areas, including possible acquisitions. Marko in particular believed that would be a big distraction. We were agreed, though, about AAPT's future being under review. We were interested in the possibility of participating in a consolidation play in the Australian market, combining in some way with other smaller players to create a larger company.

Following his announcement of the forthcoming 'stocktake', in January 2006 and during the next few months we had several meetings with David Cunliffe. In all those meetings David's focus was on investment. He never once mentioned operational separation of Telecom, like the British Telecom model, or the possibility of structural separation. Structural separation means the company being split into two completely separate companies listed on the stock market, one a retail business and one a network business, with completely separate boards and different owners. Operational separation means remaining one company with one board of directors but keeping the retail and network businesses at arm's length, with limited or no vertical integration, i.e. the retail company is not able to gain any benefits from offering services over the network it owns. The company still owns the network but rules prescribe what they can do with it.

David never said to me that either option was a possibility for Telecom New Zealand. In fact, he was very encouraging of us proceeding with our wholesale charter, on which we had briefed him before Christmas, in order to create a more level playing field for our wholesale customers, because he said that was a very difficult area for the government to address. The consistent message in every conversation and meeting he had with me was his desire to encourage more investment.

We made detailed presentations to David Cunliffe on the topic of the economics of broadband and the costs of various options. From a due process perspective, the stocktake was a shocker. It was totally unclear what the key driver really was. In one meeting, quite frustrated, my team and I asked David what the government's priorities were: Encouraging all dial-up customers to go on to broadband? Getting broadband available to as close to 100 per cent of the population as possible? Getting faster broadband into the areas where the technology made that possible? Reducing prices in the residential market? Or reducing prices in the business market? It was simply not possible for us to focus on all of those things simultaneously — there weren't enough resources. He acknowledged that this was a very good question but we never received an answer. In hindsight I believe it suited Cunliffe to make any definition of success a moving target. To set clear priorities which Telecom then responded to would have removed his justification for taking out 'the big stick'.

On the basis of the dialogue that we were having, we wrote to David after a meeting in late March and offered our commitment to a much higher broadband connection target, extending the Kiwi Share to broadband, bringing fibre to the neighbourhood by shortening local copper loops (which is the biggest driver of broadband speed and quality), connecting all small towns by fibre networks, extending coverage of DSL (Digital Subscriber Line, a technology for bringing high-speed internet to homes and small businesses over existing copper telephone lines) and agreeing that the telecommunications services obligation loss (commonly known as the Kiwi Share loss) would be set at zero, i.e. we would not seek any Kiwi Share loss contributions from other telecommunications companies as we were able to do by law. We also offered to accept Commerce Commission monitoring of our wholesale charter so that what we provided wholesale customers was completely transparent and we were accountable for it. In return for this we simply asked for a fair, stable and pro-investment regulatory regime. This was a very significant offer to table. There was certainly much debate inside Telecom about whether we should put forward something so comprehensive. I believed it was important that we put something on the table that was extensive and covered all the bases and offered a credible way forward for the government and Telecom to work together. I doubt if many people were or are today aware of the extensive nature of what Telecom was proposing.

Around this time I called Mike Williams, president of the Labour Party. He never returned my call. Funny that. I didn't hear from Mike again until more than a year later, in my last few months at Telecom, when he called to ask me, among other things, whether I was interested in being a parliamentary candidate for the party. Given how let down I felt by the actions, and in some cases the inaction, of some of his colleagues, I was completely flabbergasted. I have been flabbergasted many times in my life, but this one really took the cake.

Meanwhile, throughout this period pressure was ratcheting up in the media. In February 2006 I did a TV interview with John Campbell on *Campbell Live*. Telecom was a sponsor of the programme, which presented an obvious difficulty when it came to John interviewing me, and I think he was particularly concerned to make sure that the interview was clearly independent of the sponsor. It was a tough interview but John was courteous as always. He wasn't the problem, however. As I sat in the green room watching the start of the piece, in which he interviewed David Cunliffe, I had a deep sense of foreboding. The hostility that I saw was a far cry from the very constructive dialogue we'd always enjoyed.

As journalist Tom Pullar-Strecker wrote in the *The Dominion-Post*, 'It's hard not to come to the conclusion that Communications Minister David Cunliffe has long made up his mind that he would try and finish the job Paul Swain tried to start two years ago and impose tougher regulation on Telecom — regardless of the outcome of the "stocktake" now being undertaken by the Economic Development Ministry. An assessment of the competitiveness of broadband in New Zealand conducted at his behest by the Economic Development Ministry late last year indicated broadband was widely available and relatively cheap to consumers. Mr Cunliffe has said he will consider other metrics than those discussed by the Ministry to date. This has created the impression he is fishing for the facts to back up a desire to regulate.'[25]

And this at around the same time from Rod Oram: 'The debate has turned hysterical thanks to malicious misinformation from the use of elderly data. For example Telecom is accused of spending so little that New Zealand is near the bottom of OECD ranking on Telecom's capital expenditure, but that is based on 2001–2003 data when the rest of the world was unwisely caught up in the wildly uneconomic investment frenzy. We avoided that blow-out. Since then Telecom's New Zealand capital expenditure (excluding mobile) has risen from $232 million in the June 2002 year to $470 million this financial year. Its total spending is now 12.5 per cent of revenue, better than Europe and Asia but behind North America. Late last year, our entry-level broadband prices were the sixth lowest in the OECD and prices have fallen further since. The Government should resist the knee jerk Kiwi thing of ripping up a decent regulatory system without giving it a chance to refine and improve.'[26]

In no way were Tom Pullar-Strecker or Rod Oram in Telecom's 'pocket'. Rod in particular regularly gave Telecom a serve when he thought it was deserved. They were both knowledgeable about the subject matter, thought deeply about the issues and were resistant to pretty much everybody's particular 'spin'.

Things were definitely changing for me personally at this stage. Simon Moutter and his family had come to stay with me for an enjoyable few days at Waihi Beach over the 2005–2006 New Year period. One day we were walking along the beach talking about what we needed to do in terms of reorganising the company to meet the challenges ahead of us, and for the first time I realised that I didn't have my previous enthusiasm. At the time I became CEO and again a couple of years later, I had publicly said that I saw my timeframe in the role as five to seven years, and I was now coming up to my seventh year. The issues were becoming repetitive and felt unsolvable — how to increase profits when margins were already high, how to satisfy customers who wanted faster broadband at lower prices when the economics of deploying it were so poor, and how to extract value from the Australian business.

At a regular board meeting early in 2006 we discussed succession planning. I informed the board that I saw myself in the CEO role for only another one to two years at the most. There's no doubt that at that time the view was that my most likely successor would be an internal one — either Marko or Simon.

Meanwhile the rhythm of my weeks in both New Zealand and Australia continued. Some time after Fairfax bought Trade Me in March 2006, Chris Anderson, formerly CEO of Optus but then at Australian media company PBL, called me to ask if I'd come and meet him and James Packer, PBL's chairman. Marko and I went to their digs at Park Street, Sydney, to be met by James, Chris and John Alexander — the entire top brass of PBL — whereupon they started to aggressively question us about why we hadn't bid for Trade Me. We pointed out that Fairfax had paid an absolute fortune for it. During the course of the meeting James accused me of being aggressive. You could have knocked me down with a feather!

Marko and I were left none the wiser about the purpose of the meeting, although we thought it may have been to suss out whether we would be interested in buying PBL's New Zealand media assets. If that was the agenda it was covert rather than overt. Anyway, we had a good giggle walking back about James Packer asserting that I was aggressive, as did Roderick when I relayed the story to him. I'd actually met James before, at an earlier lunch with Peter Yates when Peter was CEO of PBL.

I well remember dining with Peter the week in April 2001 that his appointment as CEO of PBL had been announced. The media couldn't get enough of the story of how an investment banker had become a publicly listed company CEO. I'd first met Peter when he was at investment bank Macquarie with whom Telecom was working, and we'd stayed in touch. I expected Peter to be delighted about his appointment as CEO, which he was. I was startled, though, when he said, 'You know, TG, one of the great things is that I've secured a fantastic exit deal. The bride never looks as good as on the wedding day,' he explained. 'All CEO gigs end eventually and it's best to provide for that eventuality up front when they desperately want you.' I found this astonishing, but it was a very realistic approach and a strategy I now recommend to all aspiring CEOs!

In March 2006 I flew to Tokyo with Mark Flesher, our head of investor relations. Mark, whom everyone calls Flesh, had long been trying to crack the Japanese market as a source of new investors for Telecom and this trip had been planned for some time, so I did it even though things were clearly pretty tumultuous in New Zealand with the upcoming telecommunications 'stocktake', whatever that meant, on an uncertain path with uncertain timing. We were lucky enough to be in Tokyo in blossom season, those few weeks of the year when the city is bathed in beautiful blossoms. Tokyo is an amazing place because there are so many people and yet everyone is so very careful about personal space. And of course everything is beautifully arranged — going into a department store was like walking through the most exquisite gallery where, as soon as you had touched an article, a shop assistant would come along and quietly make it perfect again as you moved on.

The investor presentations we did in Tokyo were about as far a cry from the investor presentations I was used to in New York or Australia as one could imagine. At one particular lunch presentation, we walked in and sat down behind a small table, then bento boxes of food were brought to us. One by one the Japanese investors came in and were given identical bento boxes. They sat saying nothing, just eating. Then, as if on cue, everybody finished eating about the same time, put their bento boxes aside without saying a word, and waited for me to begin.

During the presentation there were no interjections, no questions. There was complete stillness in the room — indeed, one or two of the all-male audience nodded off! The only thing worse than talking when nobody is listening to you is talking to a group where you can't tell whether they're listening to you or not, and one by one they're going to sleep. When I finished and asked for questions I didn't anticipate any. However, to my surprise the questions were insightful and relevant, although very polite. That was definitely a different sort of investor meeting!

Flesh is a delightful travelling companion, and we managed to go to one of the new shopping areas where a Prada store had recently opened. I was amazed to find a pair of shoes that fitted me. My previous trip to Tokyo had been marked by my purchasing nothing more than a wallet because, being tall and curvy, with normal Western woman's-size feet, there was no way I could squeeze into any of the merchandise on sale. Shoes are a weakness of mine, and I was so delighted to be in Japan and able to fit something that I paid a ridiculous amount of money for a pair of shoes that I have never worn since because they're hugely high heeled and difficult to walk in. Still, it was exciting at the time to worship at the temple of Prada! I look back on this trip as a bright spot before things took a turn for the worse.

the beginning
of the end

It would be no exaggeration to say that life as I had known it ended on Wednesday, May 3, 2006. Tuesday, May 2 had been a great day: I had driven to the Waikato to speak at the New Zealand Large Herds (dairy) conference and decided on the spur of the moment to go to see Bella Mia, a race horse which I owned in a partnership syndicate with the Todds. I was having trouble finding their house, so I called Caroline Todd on her mobile and she met me in the middle of a deserted Cambridge road. We had a quick chinwag and then I was off to speak at the conference. I shared the platform with John Palmer, professional director, probably best known for chairing Air New Zealand, and Andrew Ferrier, Fonterra chief executive, and I answered a range of questions on leadership, integrity and resilience. Little did I know how soon I was to be tested on all of these.

I drove back to Auckland that night and flew to Australia on the Wednesday morning for a two-day board meeting and the quarterly profit announcement on Friday. When I landed, there was a message on my phone from Chris Woodwiss who was already in the Sydney office, saying that Mark Verbiest, Telecom's group general counsel, was walking around with a very furrowed brow and needed to speak to me urgently.

I called Mark as I got into the car travelling from the airport to the office. Mark was always a pleasure to work with — calm, considered, a lawyer with sound commercial judgement. On this day, though, he was deeply concerned. He said that we had a copy of a paper from David Cunliffe to Helen Clark asking permission to take through either Cabinet or Cabinet policy committee a series of proposals with relation to telecommunications regulation, which from our perspective were really bad. The paper had come to us through Peter Garty, Telecom financial controller, who had been given it by a friend from a Johnsonville cycling club who was a messenger at Parliament. Peter had briefly glanced at the cover of the document late at night, looked at it again first thing in the morning, and realising its significance immediately went to David Knight, a Telecom senior lawyer, who straight away alerted Mark Verbiest, who was himself flying to Australia for the board meeting.

I couldn't understand it, because just that Monday, May 1, as part of our ongoing dialogue, I had been on a teleconference with David at his request to discuss our proposal for working with the government to accelerate the roll-out of broadband. This Cabinet paper was dated the previous week, before that teleconference. Several other people, including Mark Verbiest, had been on that teleconference call also.

We were shocked about the contents and tone of the paper, which recommended unbundling, naked DSL (a DSL service provided without the need for the customer to purchase telephone services) and a form of separation for Telecom; either accounting separation, operational separation between retail, network and wholesale, or full structural separation, i.e. creating two completely separate companies. But more immediately we were concerned about the fact that we even *had* the paper. On the way into the city, I discussed with Mark whether we had a legal disclosure obligation. (Companies listed on the sharemarket are subject to disclosure rules, so that at all times that the market is trading, people who might wish to buy or sell Telecom shares are fully informed of any materially significant information that would impact on the share price.) We concluded that we might well have a disclosure issue, but that it depended on the status of the paper.

As soon as I arrived at the Sydney office I met with Mark and Marko Bogoievski, who was also there for the board meeting on Wednesday and Thursday and the profit announcement on Friday. We rang Pip Greenwood of Russell McVeagh to get an external legal opinion. Her view was that if the paper represented government's intended policy we would have an immediate disclosure issue and that we urgently needed to ascertain the status of the paper.

Roderick was also already at the Sydney office and we talked to him immediately. We decided that I would call David Cunliffe and attempt to ascertain the paper's status. John Goulter, my head of communications, then called the Prime Minister's chief of staff, Heather Simpson, to tell her that I was trying to get hold of David. I also rang Maarten Wevers, head of the PM's department, who wasn't available to speak to me and never returned my call.

We also discussed the issue with the board. One board member's view was that we should just give the paper back to the government. Mark Verbiest patiently explained that this would not have absolved us of the disclosure issue.

Heather Simpson then rang John Goulter back, very agitated, saying if we were going to act like this, how could anyone trust us, and that there wasn't a disclosure issue. We decided then that I would call and leave a message on Helen Clark's mobile phone, making it clear that we were not trying to create a problem or embarrass the government in any way, but that we had a legal obligation to meet.

Just before 3pm Australian time David Cunliffe returned my call and said he was about to hold a press conference in which he would be releasing the results of the stocktake, not saying anything directly about the policy paper. Our worst fears were then realised: they were serious about a very interventionist package. We knew this would send the Telecom share price crashing because no one expected the government to change course so suddenly from a light-handed regulatory framework to such an interventionist one.

It was a terrible afternoon, dashing in and out of the board meeting. At one stage a board member described it as a hiccup and said that the meeting must continue! That night I could barely stand to go to the board cocktail function with senior Australian staff. At one point a board member said to me, 'Theresa, I know you feel terrible about this, but it was 90 per cent inevitable. The defining event was this government being re-elected for a third term.'

The board meeting carried on the following day, although I was reeling from the shock of what was happening. On the Friday morning Marko and I fronted the analysts and the media at our quarterly financial results announcement. One fund manager sat in the front row and immediately asked who was accountable in terms of board and management. They were angry about the share price fall following the government's announcement, and also that we'd failed to get a deal done for Telecom's Australian business. I felt I did pretty well dealing with the analysts and my team thought so too, but some media wrote that I seemed rattled. It would have been hard not to be. On Monday, May 1, the share price was $5.66. By Friday, May 5, it had fallen to $4.64. The government's hostility was almost palpable. An Australian business journalist called me to ask me why the government hated us so much. Why indeed? Even today, a few years later, I still find what amounted to a government assault on a private company like that staggering.

The irony was that Roderick and I had regularly discussed Telstra Australia and its CEO, Sol Trujillo's, aggressive approach towards the Australian government, which looked to be working for a while, and had concluded that no good could come of it. Here we were taking great care never to criticise government policy or indeed the government at all — although Roderick and I were both often given the platform to do just that — joining organisations they asked us to (in Roderick's case, chair of the Te Papa Museum Board and in my case the Growth and Innovation Advisory Board) and, most importantly of all, genuinely trying to find a way to work together over broadband. In the end, if you look at where Telecom and Telstra are today, it made no difference.

One of the lessons, of course, is that in a regulated sector you can never put a full stop to regulation, which can sometimes lurch in unexpected directions. Marko and I had dinner that night in Sydney, still trying to make sense of things. At that point Marko was still relatively upbeat — he thought it was a puzzle that would have a solution and was definitely up for the challenge of trying to figure it out.

When I came back to New Zealand the next day, the media that greeted me was awful. *The Dominion-Post* had a horrible front-page photo of me and the *Herald* stories were nasty.

The focus in those first few days was the leaking of the Cabinet paper. The climate was so whipped up it seemed that everyone assumed Telecom had done something unethical to obtain the document. Throughout this time, politicians were attacking Peter Garty in Parliament. All we could do was tell our story to the State Services Commission, which was conducting an inquiry into how it had happened. Peter Garty was very distressed during this period, as anyone in his position would be, stressed by the journalists camping on the doorstep of his home, upset for his friend who had inappropriately given him the document, upset for himself and his family. I had a great deal of compassion for him. There may have been a few among us who would have had the presence of mind to not have accepted that envelope in the first place, but I think that most people would have taken a document from a friend and opened it. Of course, then the damage was done and taking it to a lawyer was the right course of action.

I rang Trisha McEwan over the weekend and we agreed on the need to get the executive team in one place as soon as possible. Mark Ratcliffe couldn't come to Auckland for family reasons, but Trisha,

Marko, Mark Verbiest, Chris Woodwiss and I flew to Auckland and together with my general manager – consumer Kevin Kenrick, the team met in Simon Moutter's office to talk about how we felt about the situation and what we should do. At that stage Simon was in quite a bad way — he felt very upset about what had happened and very down about his sense of purpose and belief in the business.

Marko still saw it as an intellectual challenge. Kevin and Mark Ratcliffe in particular were definitely up for taking on the new environment, so we asked them to lead the renewal project, because we knew we would have to start reconfiguring the company to deal with the contents of the announcement.

I felt like we were being attacked on all fronts. The following Monday afternoon, John Goulter came to see me in my office to say that media commentator Russell Brown had posted something on his website from an analysts' day back in March, about tele-communications companies' marketing confusing customers. I had talked about the need to simplify Telecom's pricing structures, and acknowledged that telecommunications pricing, being confusing as it often was, had contributed to keeping telco margins high. I very explicitly pointed out that this was not good enough and that we wanted to be much simpler and clearer in pricing. I put this in the context of a broader set of comments about Telecom's need to do a better job connecting with customers. All this was posted on the Telecom website at the time of the presentation and if anyone from the government had even noticed any of the comments they certainly made no response about it any time between March and the May move against Telecom. I had met David Cunliffe twice in late March after the briefing and he certainly didn't raise it with me. Some media played it up as an example of Telecom in general and its CEO in particular being very un-customer-focused. In fact, I was trying to make the very opposite point, which a few commentators picked up on, but their voices were drowned out in the barrage of negative sentiment. Now, this got new traction in the media over the next couple of days and the Prime Minister was drawn into the debate, saying she thought my comments were inappropriate.

I was very upset about being criticised for being straight up. I was pointing out that telcos all around the world have complex pricing models and saying that we were committed to changing that. I was making a frank observation about the current situation and the need for change, which was instead interpreted as endorsing that approach.

I could have chosen to go to the media and defend myself but there's no way that any interview I gave would have stuck to that topic — it would have got onto the broader issue of government intervention. By now it was obvious that telecommunications regulation was intended to be part of the upcoming budget and the leak had left a rather large hole for the government to deal with. As we were still formulating our overall response, if I went to the media at all I'd have to talk about the government's moves. However, I regret to this day that I didn't defend myself, because the whole analysts' day speech as it was on our website made it clear what I was talking about in a way that one sentence taken out of context can never do. I found it shocking, though, that honest comments could be so criticised, so maligned, in an age where honesty is held to be one of the highest virtues of anyone holding public office.

On the Wednesday night, Roderick and I talked about the need to do something to break out of the barrage of negative media and start conveying some positive messages. There was a board meeting that Thursday afternoon, but I didn't even know about it until I rang a board member, only to be told by his office that he was in a Telecom board meeting! While it was not surprising that the board was meeting to discuss the crisis engulfing the company, meeting without me could only mean one thing — they were discussing me, among other things. Still in a form of shock and almost shaking, late that afternoon I went upstairs to Roderick's office, at his request. I was worried that I was going to be fired and had already determined I wasn't going to go quietly. Instead, Roderick wanted to discuss a media release the board wanted to put out the next day about how the company was moving forward. Physically, I almost couldn't deal with coming down from being so charged with adrenaline.

As I went back to my office Mark Verbiest called to see if I was okay and I was so upset and incoherent I could barely speak to him. Concerned, he came back to the office — it was after 7pm by then and everyone had left for the night. When he came into my office I collapsed and he held me up and stopped me falling to the floor.

I went from there to Margaret Doucas's house, where she cooked me dinner and I gradually pulled myself together. I knew I had to, because of all the media I would be facing the next day when we issued the press release. I had asked Mark Ratcliffe and Kevin Kenrick to join me for the media session, following advice Kevin Roberts had given me: using a rugby analogy, he said it's much harder to take down the entire All Black team than to take down the captain.

What I gleaned later was that the board did indeed discuss my leadership of the company. They would have been well aware I had the strong support of the executive team and the wider company, and that I would never quit at the company's darkest hour. They clearly determined that stability was the most pressing need, alongside starting to regroup.

Between Wednesday, May 3, the day the Minister of Communications held his press conference, and Friday, May 5, Telecom's shares fell 90c, which equated to $1.8 billion being wiped from the market value of New Zealand's largest listed company. Leaving aside the way that it came to light, the actual contents of the government package were worse than the market expected because structural separation was put in the frame. Investors realised what we realised: at the very least the company would have to spend millions putting any new structure in place — a telco is not just a network in the ground, it's all the layers of IT systems and support that go with it. Telecom would be completely distracted from competing in the market during this time, and when separation was achieved it would be completely bound up in rules about what it could and couldn't do. In particular analysts were concerned that structural separation might lead to the government imposing a regulated rate of return on the network business.

A select committee was asked to look at both operational and structural separation, with officials from the Ministry of Economic Development working on the options. That was the biggest problem with overseas investors: unbundling and naked DSL looked like regular telecommunications policies, but this particular government's preparedness to go further than that without giving those policies a chance to deliver was very unsettling.

Once we were over the initial media shock, I realised that the next set of problems would come from investors, so Marko and I arranged to meet with investors in Auckland, Wellington and Sydney over the next 10 days. Those meetings were very difficult and took place amid media speculation about the security of my tenure. The executive team itself was still in shock and so was I.

The share price fall following the government announcement told us the market expected our profits to be lower, at least in the short term. We believed the best course of action was to embrace the new regime and to clearly win because customers chose Telecom on a level playing field. We also thought it was an important part of the new order that the Telecommunications Commissioner be front and centre, otherwise we could end up with a complete mess, i.e. trying to achieve commercial outcomes when our wholesale customers all wanted different things. We wanted a strong Telecommunications Commissioner who could send a clear ruling that everyone had to abide by. In that regard it was unhelpful that the Prime Minister came out and overtly criticised Douglas Webb. And on top of everything else, on Monday, May 1, the Commerce Commission had recommended regulation of the mobile business, which created yet more uncertainty.

Roderick made it clear that the management team and I had the full backing of the board to see the company through the coming changes. He also indicated that he would soon make an announcement about when he would retire as chairman. Shortly after this, he announced that he would retire in June.

At the time, it was reported that he'd been planning to finish as chairman for some time but his decision was precipitated by the government's plans, and I think that was a fair reading of the situation. For over two years Roderick had been concerned to put in place a clear succession for both himself as chairman and me as CEO, and in the months prior to May he had been actively mulling over leading a slightly more balanced life and scaling back his corporate commitments. Telecom and the ANZ were the two boards from which he decided to retire.

Roderick had led the recruitment process of two new directors back in early 2004, with the idea that either one of them could step up to being chairman within a couple of years. At the board meeting on June 1, 2006 Wayne Boyd was elected chairman.

When Roderick left it was the end of an era. Very few people would have taken a risk on appointing a 37-year-old woman to run New Zealand's largest publicly listed company. I never stopped appreciating Roderick for that. And Roderick was very good at the 'mechanics' of being a chairman — running a good meeting, focusing a board on the important topics, getting to the essence of an issue. For someone who holds strong views about pretty much everything, he is a surprisingly good listener.

Nevertheless we had a complex relationship — it was never the straightforward 'mentor–mentee' relationship it was often portrayed to be. While we could, and did, discuss pretty much anything in private in an open and constructive way, in more public settings we sometimes both wanted to lead the parade, which meant I often had to bite my tongue, something I didn't find easy to do. There were times of real tension between us, especially towards the end of our time working together. On the whole though, it was a relationship characterised by support, mutual respect and genuine affection.

When Wayne Boyd was announced as chairman he was immediately asked about me. We'd always got on extremely well and

I saw no difficulties in working with him as chairman but he didn't give me quite the endorsement I expected, saying only that he had confidence in the management team and avoiding making any direct reference to me at all. I think he spent the first few weeks of June widely taking soundings on my leadership before we settled into a comfortable pattern of working together, and I continued to feel very much under pressure throughout this period.

The report of the State Services Commission on the investigation into disclosure of the classified telecommunications stocktake was completed on May 16. It found that the Cabinet document had been deliberately taken from the Department of the Prime Minister and Cabinet by a messenger employed by the department and given to Peter Garty; that Peter Garty and ultimately Telecom were the passive recipients of the document, having taken no action to seek it or to encourage the messenger to provide it. They determined that having received and viewed the document, Peter Garty was immediately compromised, and that neither Peter Garty nor Telecom was at any fault in the acquisition of the document.

The two weeks between the leak and the publication of the result of the investigation were agonising. We knew that this is what had occurred from our own internal investigation, but it would have been inappropriate to say anything given that State Services was looking into it. The publicly aired assertion that we had the option of quietly handing the paper back was ridiculous. We were not a political party; we were a public company subject to all the legal requirements of disclosure for directors and senior executives. We desperately didn't want to have to disclose, but we had no choice if it was confirmed that the paper was actually government policy. Who could have foreseen that a messenger who had never previously done anything like this would have, out of some misguided notion of friendship, delivered a copy to a good mate who worked at Telecom? But ultimately, of course, it was just a sideshow. The leak simply precipitated what the government had intended to announce as part of their budget package.

On Wednesday, May 24, I had a TUANZ presentation that

I had agreed to many months prior. I knew there would be a very unsympathetic, perhaps hostile, audience but I did not want to back out or find an excuse not to present. I was fortunate to have two close girlfriends come around for dinner the night before to help me compose myself.

After David Cunliffe dropped his bombshell, the pressure on me remained intense all through June, particularly as the share price kept falling. All told, $3 billion was wiped off the value of Telecom following the announcement of the government's decision to regulate. It was still uncertain just what form that regulation would take, except it was obviously going to be bad for the company's profits.

The market is unsentimental. It looks at the company's cashflow and its likelihood of maintaining or increasing its profits into the future. It doesn't really concern itself with the context or the other stakeholders' perspectives; it votes with its feet and that's what investors were doing. There was no compelling reason to buy Telecom shares while there was so much regulatory uncertainty.

This was mainly to do with what form of separation would be required, and also the Commerce Commission's recommendation to regulate mobile on top of everything else. Not surprisingly there were some people who didn't want to see me stay: fund managers who were angry that they'd lost value in their portfolios, and competitors who saw it as a good opportunity to destabilise Telecom and its management team. Most of these people weren't named in the media articles, of course. It's easy to say what you like hiding behind a cloak of anonymity. But there were supporters, too. For example Bruce Sheppard, chairman of the New Zealand Shareholders Association, said in his colloquial way with regard to Roderick leaving that it would be dangerous to throw out the crew as well as the captain. There were also some fund managers who were prepared to be quoted as saying that making a lot of changes to board and management at that time would be entirely the wrong thing to do.

I also had support from a surprising source: Paul Budde, an

Australian telecommunications analyst who'd long been an opponent of Telecom, said my leaving would be a real pity: 'She's a great talent in communications, it would really not be a wise thing for New Zealand to do.'[27] Nobody was more surprised to read that from him than me.

I was 44 before it happened, but now I became the Gattung daughter needing the most parental support. My three sisters all had children and my mother was always available to assist them in their times of need. Mum and I had always had a good relationship and as she liked travelling, we often went on short holidays together. She particularly liked coming to Queenstown with me and going to Sydney. We never discussed anything much about work when I was marching on in my career; when someone asked her once what I did, she said, 'Well, I don't really know, but she spends a lot of time in meetings.'

Within a few days of the crisis breaking in May 2006, she was very concerned for me and came down to stay with me and cook for and generally look after me. I can remember being with her in the kitchen of my apartment reading the morning paper the day there was an editorial calling for me to go. I was glad she was there to support me, even though she felt powerless.

In their pursuit of yet more copy, newspapers went beyond the normal suspects of fund managers and telco commentators to also seek comment from headhunters. There was the 'for' camp, saying how highly regarded I was, the less enamoured camp and the 'anti' camp.

One journalist in particular went for me during June: Peter Nowak, a Canadian at that stage living in New Zealand and working as a journalist for the *Herald*. I didn't understand the source of his hostility, except perhaps the analogy that if the dragon was being slain, how could you be sure it was dead if the dragon handler was still there? But if the dragon was slain and the maiden was saved, what was the maiden? More investment in broadband?

David Cunliffe's cabinet policy paper had estimated there would be an extra $2 billion invested in broadband in New Zealand over five years from players other than Telecom, as a result of the new regulations related to fixed-line telecommunications services. Since that time (2006) little of that non-Telecom fixed-line investment has occurred — a small amount related to unbundling, principally by Vodafone and Orcon, and some fibre investment by the likes of FX Networks — but it would add up to tens of millions, not even hundreds. No one beyond Telecom has invested serious cash. Indeed, in August 2009 Telecom New Zealand's biggest competitor in the fixed-line area, TelstraClear, told the market that they had invested *less* in capital expenditure that financial year, i.e. between July 2008 and June 2009, than the previous one!

Did Cunliffe really believe there would be an extra $2 billion of non-Telecom investment arising from the proposed changes? It seems hard to fathom. David is a highly intelligent person and we had spent hours poring over the economics of broadband with him.

Interestingly, in a speech to the Korea, Australia and New Zealand Broadband Summit in June 2008 in Seoul, South Korea, Cunliffe noted that offering competing facilities-based services over the existing infrastructure (i.e. unbundling) was only going to take things so far. New Zealand also needed increased investment in that infrastructure, 'beginning with shortening loops in order to make fibre to the premise a viable prospect for the future'. How about that? The very thing we had offered more than two years previously!

During this time we had publicly said that we would do our best to make the new regime work. We sent Mark Ratcliffe, Bruce Parkes and Trisha McEwan to the UK to look at British Telecom to see how it had responded to similar pressure. BT was the one and only other telco in the world to have undergone operational separation, in September 2005, following months of negotiation with Ofcom, the UK telecommunications regulator. We also attempted to set up working parties to coordinate the technical standards, details and implementation plans for competitors to access Telecom's network even though the legislation itself was some time away from being passed.

This was a very difficult period for us. Everyone from the board down was desperate to get out of the glare of the negative media spotlight, to try to get some stability and certainty back. Incredibly, we still had no idea what the government wanted us to deliver to avoid a draconian form of separation. This played pivotally into the hands of our competitors, who had no incentive to cooperate or invest. By playing this game they could perpetuate the view of Telecom as a villain, and while the government took every opportunity to heap praise on the BT model, in reality the paint job was barely dry on the vans for its new, separated Openreach network division. Sometimes it seemed as though it was presented as if it was already clear that operational separation was the ultimate answer to the complex issues of markets and regulations in telecommunications, when really only one company in the world had gone down that path and then only very recently, too recently for any conclusions to be drawn other than the jury was still out.

On Tuesday, June 13, Wayne, the executive team and I gathered in Auckland to discuss the way forward in terms of the need to move to operational separation. I felt good at the beginning of that meeting, as we were starting to put together a concrete plan to work within the new order. I have been asked since whether we ever contemplated the equivalent of civil disobedience (i.e. just not obeying the government's recommendations) and the answer is no; we never considered something that would so obviously have been a disaster for our customers. We saw ourselves as a business serving customers — we didn't see ourselves as an institution with a separate life like, say, a political party with an ideological agenda.

However, part-way through that meeting John Goulter sent me an email saying *The Independent* was going with a story the next day saying that my relationship with Helen Clark was at an all-time low, which plunged me down again. I thought we had turned the corner and now there was going to be another unhelpful media piece. I regathered my composure in the meeting because I could hardly sit there for the next few hours and be passive, worried about my own issues. I had to be the leader, and I was.

Sure enough, it was the front-page *Independent* story on June 14,[28] quoting unnamed Labour Party insiders saying that there had been a breakdown in my relationship with the government and that it had become deeply personal for Helen Clark. Obviously at this point Helen wasn't calling me for chats as she had once done, but things never got personal between us and I was disappointed that her office didn't do more to play down that story. (The same insider opined in this piece that Telecom had had the option of quietly handing the policy paper back but chose to embarrass the government by not exercising that option. As I've said previously, Telecom had no option of quietly handing the paper back. Unfortunately, once it was passed to us we had no alternative but to ascertain its status and the rest, as they say, is history.)

Although Helen Clark and I were never really close, we had always got on well and we had quite a few points of connection. We were both strong feminists who understood how much harder it was for women than men to get to the top of their respective fields and stay there, and we respected each other for that. We also met at several women's events, such as the launch of the Auckland YWCA mentoring programme for women at which we were both guest speakers, and her parents lived at Waihi Beach, where John and I had had a beach house for many years. The truth of the matter from my perspective was that we were never as close as some people believed at certain times, but nor did we fall out in the way that was later reported.

Over that week we tried to get a telecommunications industry working group proposal off the ground and had a frustrating few days trying to get support for it. It seemed like certain competitors had an agenda to keep us stuck where we were.

I went back to Sydney on June 19 but everything had changed. The executive team dinner wasn't the same. We were no longer a committed bunch with shared hopes and optimism for the future — or at least that's not how I felt. Previously there had always been such a buzz just being together. Now we were all quieter, each person reflecting on the tectonic shift that had taken place and what it might mean for them.

The following week Wayne Boyd and I met with TUANZ to make it clear that we were trying to move forward. On the Tuesday afternoon, after a board meeting in the morning, Wayne and I did a media briefing together, saying that we were proposing voluntary operational separation. I then presented the proposal at the annual telecommunications summit, taking the stage after David Cunliffe had spoken, and I realised that he was very lukewarm about the idea.

One good thing that happened around this time was an afternoon tea Wayne and I had with Tony Boyd from the *Australian Financial Review* in Sydney. Tony could see we genuinely had a good relationship and that there wasn't any tension between us. After that the media speculation about my imminent departure quietened down for a while.

In late July Wayne and I also met with David Cunliffe and Michael Cullen to try to agree on a process of engaging in a transparent way to achieve operational separation. I left the meeting feeling that Michael was in support of this approach but that David was more reserved.

The following week was the August earnings announcement, and we had positioned that day to be a full presentation of our strategies. Marko had sent a great email detailing what it needed to cover and we fronted with the whole team: me, Marko, Kevin, Simon, Mark Ratcliffe and Wayne, with media packing the room to the gunwales. By the end of that week I thought I'd done as well as anyone could have done in the situation we found ourselves in.

The following week I started doing performance reviews of the senior team and I spoke at the Telecom sales conference in Auckland. I shared a little of my personal anguish over the preceding couple of months and received a fantastic response from the sales team. At drinks that evening the staff were just so wonderful and supportive.

It was undoubtedly one of the worst periods of my life to date. You read critical commentary about other people in the media all the time, but you have no idea how it feels until it happens to you, or how quickly and unfairly the media can demonise people. It really penetrated me to my core.

May and June had been the hardest two months but I had been

feeling terribly burdened since February, caught between what a leader needs to do to support others and my own need for support, with no one to go home to at night to discuss things with or to share what was going on. Normally a very optimistic person — in fact, a journalist once wrote that I could be mistaken for an author of self-help books — I was by this time starting to get very weary.

The person to whom I regularly turned for advice and counsel over this period was Kevin Roberts. It was impossible to turn to anybody within my immediate circle, consumed as they all were by the developing situation and what it meant for them. Kevin had been personally involved with the Telecom account, including working with my executive team and myself, so I knew he had a good understanding of the issues. He always had a great perspective on how to think about shareholders, customers and staff interactions and dynamics.

I'll always be grateful for the support he gave me during this period, both professionally and personally. Kevin is so busy, normally he can be difficult to reach — if you leave a message on his mobile he'll probably get back to you three days later, from a different part of the world! During this time, for long periods he left his mobile on so that he could return my calls as soon as I rang.

I believe the board supported me at this time because they could see that I had the support of the company and also because they believed that changing the chief executive at the same time as the chairman would create an impression, or certainly add to the impression, of a company in crisis.

One thing I began to do immediately was showcase the rest of the Telecom executive team as much as possible, based on Kevin Roberts's All Blacks analogy. At the August profit results Wayne and I fronted up not just with Marko as CFO but also with Kevin Kenrick, head of consumer; Simon Moutter, head of business; Mark Ratcliffe, CIO; and Matt Crockett, the new general manager – wholesale. This did help to defuse commentary about me.

In a poll of chief executives of small and large companies taken after the government telecommunications policy changes were announced, most respondents agreed with the likely outcome of the new regulation (i.e. more competition) but around half raised concerns about the method. Comments included, 'While I agree with the outcome the method used was unfortunate', 'The local loop needed freeing up but not in the way it was done' and 'The government was right to act but the way they acted was inappropriate'.[29]

Policy emerges from popular opinion and popular will. There is no doubt the New Zealand government had popular opinion and popular will on its side. But popular opinion doesn't arise in a vacuum. It had been hugely shaped by the commentary.

a forced separation

Marko, Simon, Mark Verbiest, Mark Ratcliffe, Trisha and I spent most of August debating for hours what form of operational separation would work for everyone concerned and be enduring and sustainable, before our presentation to the Finance and Expenditure Select Committee, which was charged with considering the workings of the Telecommunications Amendment Bill, which would make the government's regulation plan law. While the government had signalled its intention to open up Telecom's network to more competition, the select committee was charged with determining how this would actually work, and in particular making recommendations on accounting separation, operational separation and structural separation options. Shane Jones was the chairman.

During this period our support for each other was unwavering, but different views did start to emerge in terms of how we thought the company should best approach the situation we found ourselves in. Simon thought there needed to be a complete circuit breaker to change the nature of the conversation with the government. Marko was getting increasingly concerned about whether any model of operational separation was sustainable. He saw it as imposing a huge deadweight cost on the whole industry, benefitting neither Telecom nor the rest of the industry, whereas other members of the team thought that it would be manageable.

We decided that our best bet was to try to use the platform of the select committee to make it clear that we were generally getting on with life under the new rules of the game, even though it was still very uncertain exactly how it would all play out. Huge damage had been done to the brand by being so attacked and vilified in the previous few months, so we were very focused on bringing as much stability to the situation as we could for our customers and our staff.

We accepted that the government had the right to reset the ground rules but I think we should have argued that they should have compensated Telecom shareholders for taking back something a previous government — another Labour administration! — had sold. This view wouldn't have carried the day but it would have focused attention on what was really going on. There was a destruction of wealth for Telecom shareholders which the government, given its role to make decisions in what it believed were the best interests of the whole country, believed would be balanced by lower prices, specifically in broadband but also possibly other services, and more choice for consumers, thereby directly or indirectly benefitting the country by more than the value of the loss to shareholders. But in this situation the destruction of value to one group was so clear and the purported increase in economic good to another so unclear.

About this time we also came to the conclusion that although Directories (the Yellow Pages division of Telecom) was still growing and was a strong cash cow, it was likely to show lower earnings growth in the future as the business went increasingly online, and its maximum value had probably been reached. The amount of money that private-equity companies were prepared to pay for directory

Telecom NZ Ltd

Above: Me at the wheel of a New Zealand America's Cup boat with Russell Coutts, 2002. I was out on the water with them for hours and developed a better appreciation of the skill that's involved in manoeuvring those boats.

Below left: In the Telecom boardroom, 2003. I'm not sure the leather jacket was really a CEO look!

Below right: My dear friend Margaret Doucas. We have enjoyed many good times together in New Zealand, Australia and further afield, and supported each other through many hard times.

Telecom NZ Ltd

Evening Post

Above: Me at Waihi Beach, 2004. I think of Waihi as my 'spiritual home'.

Right: John and me at Waihi Beach, Easter 2005, a week before our separation.

Below: Mum and Dad left Rotorua many years ago for the warmer climate of the Western Bay of Plenty. Here I am with them at Ohope beach, 2004.

John Savage

Simon Wilson

Joanne Black

Guy Body, *New Zealand Herald*

Telecom NZ Ltd

Above: A cartoon of Helen Clark, Ann Sherry, then Westpac CEO, and me, July 31, 2004. This cartoon, which took up almost all of the front page of the *Weekend Herald* business section, led into a story headlined 'Word in Your Ear, Ma'am', that discussed which businesspeople had the government's ear and said I was 'the best example of the type of pragmatic business leader that has managed to build a good relationship with the Clark government'. Helen's business buddies were listed as me, Ann Sherry, Creative New Zealand head Peter Biggs, the Growth and Innovation Advisory Board's Rick Christie, McKinsey's Andrew Grant and Fletcher Building's Ralph Waters.

Left: In my office at Telecom, 2005. Although I like the colours in this photo, when I look at it now, I think how strained I look during this period compared to photos from just the previous year.

APN

Above: Media packed the room in which the Finance and Expenditure Select Committee was meeting. Who knew the details of operational separation could be so interesting? Marko Bogoievski and me, with Wayne Boyd in the background, Rodney Hide at left, November 2006.

Below: This was reported as me shedding a tear at the February 2007 Telecom profit result presentation, where I announced that I was leaving Telecom at the end of the June 2007 financial year. Actually, I'm just adjusting my glasses!

APN

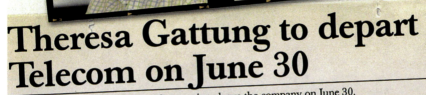

Theresa Gattung to depart Telecom on June 30

chief executive Theresa Gattung is to leave the company on June 30.
...on Friday. Ms G... Telecom's chief exec...

Telecommunications Ministe wishes Theresa Gattung wel

The Telecommunications Minister David Cunliffe has extended good wishes to Telecom's outgoing chief executive Theresa Gattung following her resignation today.

Mr Cunli... one of the... figures...

He says he had frequent contact with her in his ministerial role and th... respects her energy and passion...

The Government last year mov... to open its copp... split the compan... units, to make t...

Theresa Gattung will step down at ...nd of June and Telecom has alrea... ...ecutive search tea...

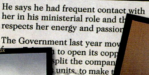

Above: A page from the wonderful farewell book my team gave me when I left Telecom in 2007. From top left: Kevin Kenrick, Marko Bogoievski, Simon Moutter, Trisha McEwan, Mark Ratcliffe, Mark Verbiest and Chris Woodwiss.

Above: Christmas Day is always a wonderful day of family and feasting, and 2007 was no exception! Here I am with my mother at my sister Marion's house.

Below left: Mum, me and my sister Yvonne at the Waikato University Alumni Awards. July 2007.

Below right: I've presented on wool to many audiences, both urban and rural. Everyone gets the importance of reinvigorating the wool industry for the good of New Zealand. This photo was taken during an interview I gave about this. January 2009.

Ken George

Jane Ussher

Above: Me outside my apartment in Wellington June 2007. I'm a real 'water baby' and love living at a city beach.

Below: The cover of *Next* magazine. March 2009.

Emma Bass, ACP Media

Above: My mother Marion Gattung is talented at embroidery. This is a tablecloth and napkin set — made with love as a gift for me, shown here with china from my vintage china collection.
Below: I really enjoy collecting vintage china and linen and giving them as gifts.

assets owned by telcos was staggering. Indeed, quite a bit earlier representatives of the very well-known, huge American private-equity firm KKR had flown to Sydney for a meeting with Marko and me to sound us out on whether we would be interested in selling our Directories business.

Despite the chaos going on around me, in late 2006 I was once again on *Fortune* magazine's list of the 50 most powerful women in international business outside the United States. I had been named in the list for the first time in 2002, then again in 2003, at number 37, moving up to number 32 in 2004. Now I'd moved up from 29th place in 2005 to 23rd place on the list. In late August 2006, *Forbes* magazine announced that I was ranked 49th on their list of the 50 most powerful women in the world across all spheres: politics, business, entertainment. The irony of having my highest-ever ranking on the *Fortune* list and having made the *Forbes* list at this time was that never had I felt less powerful in all my time as Telecom CEO.

At the time there were few dissenting voices in the breathless rush to regulate Telecom. One of the few was Victoria University academic Bronwyn Howell, who published work which, among other things, pointed out that there was no evidence linking broadband penetration with economic growth. She suggested that politicians' emphasis on broadband was similar to the hype that accompanied the dotcom bubble, saying, 'What has characterised the stocktake is the complete absence of sound empirical reasoning.'[30]

Her research indicated that in the previous year New Zealand had had the world's highest percentage of internet users, with 76 per cent of Kiwis using the net. The fact that broadband uptake was consistent with where New Zealand sat in terms of GDP per capita and not higher was best explained *not* by New Zealand not having the technology or prices being too high, but because dial-up internet was very good value, backed up by free local calling for dial-up internet users and a lack of applications that would run only on broadband. No one was interested in her findings, though. The train had already left the station.

More recently, in November 2009, a government-funded survey of 6000 firms in New Zealand by Waikato University and Motu Economic research consultancy demonstrated the same thing — there is no link between the availability of high-speed broadband and business productivity. The report uncovered a 10 per cent productivity gain where businesses first adopted broadband, but no link between broadband's speed and overall productivity.[31]

The report also said that despite well-articulated pleas for upgraded internet access, reference to rigorous research that quantified benefits actually occurring from network upgrades was generally absent. And then there was the Scribbler's take on it in that week's *National Business Review*: 'A survey of 6000 firms proves what we all knew instinctively to be true: there is no link between fast broadband and increased productivity.'[32] What we all knew instinctively to be true? There is no link between fast broadband and increased productivity? This in the same paper that barely three years prior had made it a cause célèbre to claim that Telecom's failure to invest quickly enough in high-speed broadband was holding back businesses and therefore the entire country?

While I'm sure most New Zealanders thought the changes to the telecommunications industry in 2006 were a good thing for the country because of a very deeply held belief in a level playing field and a view that Telecom was too big for its boots, operating in a business environment constantly disrupted by new technologies is not that simple. On its own, regulation doesn't spur the investment to deliver broadband at blistering speeds and low prices. That takes investor confidence and economic reward, and as I pointed out in an interview just before I finished at Telecom, if we were serious about broadband as a country we'd need a government pledge to spend at least $1.5 billion on infrastructure.[33] Not long after that National, then in opposition, announced exactly that would be one of its central campaign tenets — modelled, I believe, on a similar and successful approach by the then-opposition party in Australia. But guess what? The *how* to do it is blindingly complex and the *who* to do it appears to have got bogged down by companies such as Vector pointing out that without bigger government subsidies there's not enough return on investment for the private sector. Watching the New Zealand government decide how best to spend $1.5 billion on broadband is like watching paint dry — it seems to take forever.

The problem with broadband in New Zealand today is the same as it's always been: it's hard to make money on such a high-cost investment in such a small market. Some of the people who for years have called for Telecom to be held to account for 'holding the country back' are blind to the economics of investment in broadband, and wilfully so.

In early September Marko, Mark Ratcliffe and I made our first presentation to the select committee. It was a bit like going into a combat zone when I had never visited the location in peacetime. We made it clear that we would not oppose the bill and were committed to making the new telecommunications environment work. We outlined what we'd done since the stocktake was released: creating an independent wholesale unit, starting the drafting of a set of enforceable public and legally binding undertakings that would guarantee a level playing field between Telecom and its competitors to be overseen by the Telecommunications Commissioner and an independent oversight group, and initiating two industry working parties to work through the practical nuts and bolts of delivering the new regulated services. We also put on the table a voluntary operational separation restructuring of the company. These were the key features of BT's model.

It was hard to tell how well it went. On the whole, the MPs on the select committee were not overly aggressive in their questioning, but telecommunications is a complex business and it was clear that some of them were struggling to understand just what we were talking about.

After the presentation we got word from the select committee that they were keen to see demonstrated board support, specifically for the proposal we were tabling and more generally for a different way of working. So we presented to the select committee a second time a few weeks later, this time with Wayne Boyd, Telecom chairman, and Rob McLeod, chairman of the Telecom board's audit and finance committee. At this second session the questioning was dominated by Paul Swain and Maurice Williamson — both previous ministers of communications.

Shane Jones did a good job running the meetings but I was deeply offended when at the end of the second session he walked from one end of the table down to where Rob, Wayne and I were sitting and, as we got up to leave, hongi'd Rob and Wayne then turned on his heel and walked away. I regarded it as a deliberate insult. Symbolically it felt like my head had been cut off and I guess that was what he intended. I was surprised the media didn't notice and comment on it, or maybe they did notice and chose not to. Given that Shane and I had had previous dealings completely separate from Telecom when we had worked together on the board of a charity, it clearly was nothing personal between us. It was about me as CEO of Telecom. I found it disrespectful and completely unnecessary.

The Telecom AGM of October 2006 was subdued — how could it have been anything else? At that point Telecom had suffered a $3.3 billion drop in sharemarket value since May when the government announced its intention to heavily regulate the company. We announced at the AGM that we'd be stopping donations to political parties, which was a popular move with domestic shareholders. It had become clear that shareholders and customers did not like Kiwi companies making political donations even if they were demonstrably even-handed between the two major political parties.

In November we reported our profit for the first three months of the 2006–2007 financial year. Remarkably, despite all the time and effort and energy and focus on dealing with the regulatory interventions, the huge push we'd had in mobile and broadband the previous couple of years continued to pay off, and our profits were higher than the same quarter the previous year. We also officially announced that we were putting the Yellow Pages business up for sale, and that AAPT had struck a wholesale network deal with

Australian company PowerTel which was likely to be the first step toward a complete merger. The share price started tracking upward towards $5 again.

In late November the select committee recommended operational separation of Telecom's network, wholesale and retail businesses (as opposed to either just accounting separation, a much lesser form of separation, or full structural separation, which would mean two completely new companies with different owners). It recommended giving the Minister of Communications the power to manage the split and to exert a high degree of control over the details. Interestingly, our share price rose immediately, partly because so much bad news had already been reflected in the share price and partly because some investors thought that Telecom had dodged a bullet in that a tougher form of regulation, i.e. full structural separation, had not been recommended.

The real problem, however, was that the devil was in the detail, and that detail was going to take a while longer to work through and was entirely in the hands of the minister. The recommendation was strongly based on the British Telecom operational separation model which had been talked up ad nauseam by the government and some industry commentators. Media headlines that Telecom had been 'let off the hook on full split'[34] helped compound the view that a more benign outcome had occurred. We didn't think so. We were shattered, because we understood that it was going to impose huge costs — unnecessarily, in our opinion, as we had already offered a voluntary operational separation which would have dealt with the key issues in a much less complex way. It felt like a government hell-bent on changing the telecommunications regulatory environment once and for all (as if)!

The market at that stage saw it as an outcome tilted towards the better end of possibilities, but Marko told analysts that he believed the market was underestimating the complexity and costs of New Zealand-style separation.

But it wasn't all doom and gloom. In December it was announced that Gen-i had won a big contract to replace TelstraClear as telecommunications and information support services provider for the Ministry of Justice in a deal worth about $50 million over five years.

The same month we also launched an upgrade to the mobile broadband network which saw speeds equal to that of fixed network broadband. In the same week we announced a joint venture between Telecom and Yahoo!7, effectively replacing Telecom's five-year Xtra-MSN partnership with Microsoft. It had been a very difficult year, but when you're CEO, the show must go on.

Chapter seventeen

time
to go

Generally I spend Christmas and part of January at the beach, but at the end of a hectic 2006 I decided I needed to clear my head by going somewhere completely different. I flew to California to spend Christmas with good friends there and went on to New York for New Year and a few weeks in January. While I was away in a completely different environment, I mulled things over and I knew I would leave Telecom in June, at the end of the financial year.

I knew I couldn't stay on — it would have done my head in. Given the government's intention to impose operational separation on Telecom, I no longer believed that the company could grow its earnings and a person can't lead a publicly listed company if they don't believe that, unless they are prepared to be very cynical. And I wasn't. In addition, with Telstra's announcement that it was shutting down the CDMA network in Australia, it was obvious that we needed to shift mobile technologies again and I doubted I had the energy to undergo that process. At the February profit result we were going to announce another great quarter for mobile, marking a solid two years in which we'd outperformed Vodafone and grabbed back market share, but it would need fresh energy for the next phase.

When I became CEO, and again a couple of years after that,[35] I had indicated that I thought about seven years would be it for me, and 15 months earlier this was exactly the timing that I'd discussed with the board. And during that time, to all intents and purposes but through no desire of our own, Telecom had almost come to be treated like a political party rather than a commercial company. A fresh approach would be best demonstrated by fresh faces at the top — despite the fact that the new chairman, Wayne Boyd, had already been on the board for the previous two years! Wayne has the happy knack of blending seamlessly into new environments. (Interestingly, Alan Jury wrote recently in the *Australian Financial Review*[36] that the replacement of Telstra chair Don McGauchie and CEO Sol Trujillo, who were deemed to have fallen foul of the government, by Catherine Livingstone and David Thodey in 2009 would at best make a marginal difference around the edges in terms of the likely shape of regulation. There were few such prescient commentators in New Zealand but that has also proved to be the case here.)

My departure was to be officially announced on February 2, 2007, at the earnings announcement. The evening of February 1, sitting in my hotel room in Auckland preparing my presentation for the next day, was very lonely. With me that evening, and the next morning until I fronted the media and analysts at 10am, were a few of my close stalwarts: Chris Woodwiss, John Goulter (who himself finished at Telecom that week), Philip King, and Mark Rudder from Cosways, our communications firm in Australia. I could never thank them enough for supporting me at that time, even when there was no longer anything in it for them. I did feel a bit let down by quite a few other people, however. It was rather like the queen is dead; long live the king. Chris and I had a wry chuckle about how popular Marko had suddenly become and the queues of people lining up outside his door who just had to speak to him. Needless to say, when some months later it was announced that Paul Reynolds was going to be the next CEO those crowds dispersed.

Although it was right on the timing I'd anticipated in terms of leaving, it was not the way I'd anticipated. I was hardly going out in a blaze of glory. But after the announcement, I felt a great sense of relief that the burden was about to be lifted from my shoulders.

The next day I received hundreds of emails from Telecom staff, sad to see me go. My immediate team understood though.

Early in 2007 we announced the sale of Yellow Pages to private equity for $2.2 billion, which was 13 times the division's projected 2007–2008 EBITDA of $170 million. Roderick had never been as keen on selling the Yellow Pages business as management was and we didn't finally get board approval until after he'd left Telecom. The timing ended up being quite fortuitous in terms of the price we received. A year later a prominent New York merchant banker told me that this deal was regarded as the high-water mark of private equity deals done anywhere in the world in telecommunications over that boom period.

Apart from the very successful sale of Yellow Pages and my announcement, those first few months of 2007 were dominated by ongoing, extensive discussions and analysis on separation and the process of starting to engage with officials. Marko was the first of us to form a view that the industry more broadly, and investors specifically, would be better served by complete structural separation, where the retail and services business were owned separately from the network company, rather than the halfway house of operational separation.

Marko told a group of analysts in Sydney in March that investors were underestimating the cost and complexity of operational separation New Zealand-style. At the time he made those comments the share price was $4.80. By the time the government's changes had been implemented, the Telecom share price had fallen to under $2.30. Even allowing for the re-rating of all companies as part of the global financial downturn, it is clear that Marko was right. Of the rest of us, some thought that operational separation would indeed be manageable and others just hoped that it would be, but the more time went on and the more we delved into it, the more downbeat we all became about it.

By late March the whole executive team had become convinced that it would be much cleaner to have a complete structural split, and after extensive conversations with the board, it came to share that view. Accordingly, in mid-April we publicly presented our proposal for structural separation to the government. But within a week of the early May profit result briefing to financial analysts and media where Wayne, Marko and I reiterated this stance, the board had lost its conviction. It was an impossible situation. We couldn't have Marko and me talking to investors and the media, saying that Telecom was firmly behind structural separation, and the chairman talking to ministers saying that the company was happy to go down the path they'd outlined. So we all got together and it became obvious that there was no longer any stomach for the structural separation proposal. I believe that what happened during this period (and this was later corroborated by a reliable source) was that the board had started interviewing for CEO candidates to succeed me, and they had spoken to more than one candidate who told them what they probably wanted to hear — namely that operational separation was manageable from a shareholder-value perspective and there was no need to do something as drastic as structural separation.

In a way it didn't matter for me — because I was leaving I had no personal stake in either outcome — but it was devastating for Marko, who is an incredibly principled person. He had worked tirelessly over many months to build up the empirical data to come to a conclusion, only to see it tossed out because one or two blokes — people who'd probably done nothing more than have a quick glance at the last Telecom annual report and look at a few newspaper headlines — thought there was a better way. It was at that point that he told the board he wasn't interested in the CEO job and started making other plans.

For me it was a very turbulent, upsetting time. I think the board was in an incredibly difficult situation and that they acted as well as most boards would in that situation. There was always constructive dialogue with management — there was no fracture around the boardroom, either between board members or board and management. There was no leaking to external parties. It might have looked like a bit of a flip-flop from the outside but it didn't look like a situation of dissent. Commercially, of course, it's fair enough to assume that if you behave reasonably towards another party they will behave reasonably towards you, but this had now become all about politics, and politics is about power. I felt sad that the strategy of 'complete capitulation', as it was dubbed by one journalist, had won the day, and I doubted that it would prove to be the right approach, though at the time it was certainly a popular one.

After news of my leaving came out, both David Cunliffe and Helen Clark were quite charitable about me, but Cunliffe made the point that Telecom had been very focused on shareholder value and not very focused on its responsibilities to the country. No CEO of a company listed on the sharemarket lasts very long if they're not focused on maximising the return to their investors, and therein lies the rub. The way Telecom had been privatised, not enough Kiwis had a financial stake in its success, so I believe the public preference would have been for it to be an SOE (state-owned enterprise), with a dual purpose of being run as a business but also explicit responsibility to the country through Crown ownership and oversight by a minister.

Hardly surprisingly, I didn't enjoy the last few months in the job. When you get out of the water it closes behind you, something former broadcaster Sharon Crosbie had said to me a full 15 years earlier about her own change of career. In my case I was still in the water, but gradually being swum around as the time for my departure neared. Having been in the centre of the action and directing activities for so long, I hated the fact that the focus of power had now shifted to the chairman of the board, even though Wayne Boyd treated me well.

In March I took a break because for the first time in a very long time taking a week off during the course of the year was possible! Margaret Doucas, my friend Catherine Savage and I went to Gwinganna

Lifestyle Retreat in Queensland. Catherine was finishing as managing director of AMP in New Zealand and so was herself in a time of career transition. We'd known each other for a while and always liked each other, and we became closer friends through this time.

Gwinganna is a gorgeous place in a beautiful setting, with delicious though healthy food. However, two days into it I became violently ill, vomiting continuously for nearly 24 hours, and I felt wrung out for the next few days. I think it was my body saying enough is enough, time for a rest.

I went overseas one last time with Marko and Mark Flesher to talk to investors in May, and I was touched that a fund manager from a company that had been a strong investor in Telecom through many of its ups and downs travelled from Washington to New York to say goodbye in person. I'd have to say I was surprised how nice the fund managers were to me on that last trip, investing being a pretty unsentimental business.

Also in May we completed the takeover of PowerTel in Australia for AU$357 million. Because PowerTel owned infrastructure, buying the company was a good opportunity for AAPT to lessen its reliance on Telstra's high-priced wholesale services. We appointed the CEO of PowerTel, Paul Broad, the CEO of our Australian business.

My Auckland farewell in late June was a bit of a subdued affair, with mainly people from outside Telecom there and a space that was rather too cavernous, but my Wellington farewell was wonderful, a riotous party with barely standing room — packed with people from Telecom and other close associates. My team had compiled a video of funny moments over the years complete with comments, which was hilarious. It was a bittersweet evening for me. I felt acknowledged and warmed by people's genuine respect and affection for me, but also very sad because it was the end of an era, a huge part of my life.

Then I packed up my office and drove out of the garage for the last time. Actually, some people were surprised to see me drive out in my car because they assumed it was a company car. (I had had a company car earlier on, but after dinging it a few times I decided it was a bad look to keep sending it in for minor panelbeating, so I'd bought my own.) And off I drove to the Wairarapa for a weekend with some of my closest girlfriends. I was still sad but I was also just starting to feel excited about life after Telecom. It was time to get back on a horse.

rebuilding

Mark Weldon, chief executive of the New Zealand Stock Exchange, had told me about Estancia La Paz, one of the many horse-riding ranches in Argentina, where he and his wife Sarah had got married. This sounded like a great place to decompress. Catherine Savage and I decided to go there that August, just over a month after I'd left Telecom. I flew down from holidaying in the United States and she flew across from New Zealand.

Our adventure actually started before we got to Argentina. During our flight from Chile to Argentina there was, we both agreed later, the worst turbulence we'd ever experienced. I am normally a very good traveller and have had many rocking and rolling flights in New Zealand caused by the sometimes unpredictable wind, but this was something else again. I was quite frightened — all I could think about was a plane crash in the Andes many years earlier where the survivors had eaten their dead companions in order to stay alive! At one point I must have turned white, because the nun who was sitting next to me put her hand on my arm and said not to worry, we would all be fine. Never have I been so pleased to descend in a plane as I was when we came into Córdoba airport, about 650 kilometres northwest of Buenos Aires, near the geographical centre of Argentina.

We were picked up and driven to Estancia La Paz, about 45 kilometres north of Córdoba. The place was wonderful; a landscape of rolling hills that went on for miles and reminded me of Australia, and architecture that was clearly of European heritage. There was also very friendly service from the bilingual Spanish- and English-speaking staff, including our waiter for the week, who was called Manuel. I mean, what else would he be called? There was no email because the one PC was broken and poor cellphone coverage. Bliss!

We were welcomed by the staff with big hugs as if they were greeting long-lost friends — very nice when you turn up in a strange place feeling somewhat jet-lagged. The food was delicious, a real meat-eater's paradise. Meat for breakfast, lunch and dinner was the order of the day, topped off by the week's highlight — a particular form of Argentinean barbecue which was one delicious cut of meat after another. And everywhere were the national flag, statues of horses, books about horses and of course the real thing: lots of horses.

Estancia La Paz was owned by four brothers who kept a team of over 50 polo ponies. The horses we rode each day were retired polo ponies. They were perfectly groomed and beautifully mannered. Each day we would get up, have a sumptuous breakfast (making sure we ingested much bran for fibre to offset the meat that lay ahead), then we would go down to where the horses were corralled and Marco the gaucho would select horses for the guests who were riding. Once we found horses that were right for us we stayed with them for the week. On the first day I was given a horse that was rather too slow for me, so on the second day I was given Indian. He and I complemented each other very well and I rode him every day after that.

I was totally in my element. Horse riding is great exercise. It's much harder work than it looks, and a much more enjoyable workout than any other form of physical activity that I've ever tried. It is also the most incredible adrenalin buzz because you can never entirely control a 500 kilogram animal. You can send it messages from your brain and parts of your body, but it is quite special to be in sync together, cantering up a hill or executing difficult dressage movements. And then there's the sheer ability to cover so much distance so quickly. You can be up in the hills looking down on the city within minutes. You can enjoy it by yourself or with other people, and you get a real sense of achievement as you learn and improve. No one ever knows everything about riding and I still enjoy having regular lessons, as well as cantering over the hilltops.

I used to do quite a bit of jumping, which is also a real adrenalin buzz, but a series of minor injuries to my groin and hand meant that I haven't done it for over a year now. I am not quite ready to say that I won't do it again, but it's certainly true that as you get older your propensity to be comfortable leaving the ground on horseback does diminish — at least it has for me.

Animals can teach you a lot. I can tell within a few minutes of hopping on my horse Pride how he is feeling. Horse riding is never a mechanical thing. It is two living, breathing, sensing entities cooperating. And horses are dangerous because they're so sensitive and when anxious their instinct is flight. They're also pack animals and want to do what the other horses around them are doing.

Catherine had done less riding than me, but it didn't matter because the horses at Estancia La Paz were so well mannered. The station was so big — 2000 hectares — that each day we rode out to a different part of it, sometimes just the two of us with either one of the owners or Marco, and sometimes in a bigger group. Pretty early on we discovered a full-size polo field a few minutes' walk from the main building and we thought it would be fun to have a polo lesson. We asked the owner if he would give us one, and in halting English he asked us, 'You can ride, yes?'

'Yes,' we said. 'We've been riding.'

Then he said, 'But you can't play polo?'

'No,' we said, 'we can't play polo.'

Again he asked us, 'Do you know how to ride?'

'Yes, we can ride.'

'But you can't play polo?'

'No,' we repeated, 'we don't know how to play polo.' It became clear that in this part of the world playing polo was a natural extension of riding, and the notion of being able to ride but having never played polo seemed as strange to him as the idea of having a licence to drive a car and not regularly driving seems to us.

So we took our ponies to the polo field. They were very patient; even when I hit Indian in the head with the mallet he didn't bolt or jump sideways. As I suspected, polo was very difficult. The hand and eye coordination required to hit the ball when you're moving at speed on a horse, combined with the strength required to hit it any distance, makes for quite hard work. Nevertheless, our instructor regularly called out 'Very well, Catherine' and 'Very well, Theresa', by which we assumed he meant very good!

Actually the two of us combined would have been quite good for a beginner. Because I've done more riding I was more comfortable on horseback and more often able to coordinate actually connecting the mallet with the ball. But Catherine is a formidable tennis and badminton player and much stronger than me, and when she did connect she managed to shift it quite a lot further than I could. I realised that I didn't have quite the strength I'd had prior to breaking my wrist in that fall from my horse Spy, nearly 10 years earlier.

After riding in the mornings we'd go back to the hacienda for a late lunch and then a siesta, then we'd spend the afternoon exploring on foot or having treatments in the spa. There were a few other guests, but Catherine and I were the only people using the spa, so we had a delightful time moving backwards and forwards between the treatment rooms, having facials and massages, the spa bath and the sauna. Everything was very stylish.

It was exactly what my body needed. I was a lot more exhausted on leaving Telecom than I had realised. The stress of those last two years had caused my periods to stop. I thought I had gone into early menopause and was going to be one of approximately 20 per cent of women who have no menopausal symptoms at all, just one day their periods cease. It wasn't till many months after I'd left Telecom that my body came back into balance and my periods started again. It wasn't just the stress of the last year in the eye of the storm, or the last eight years as CEO, or the last 13 years at Telecom — it was the stress of the previous 25 years, from the time I joined TVNZ as assistant market research manager, fresh out of business school, and embarked on my rise up the corporate ladder.

Nobody in public life working under constant scrutiny is immune to stress and it eventually shows up in your body one way or another. As Bill Ralston wrote in *The Listener*, 'Those who have not been at the centre of a media furore can't understand the real tension and pressure that can be inspired by a single newspaper headline or sound grab on radio or television. When it is your life, your reputation, your career at stake, every nuance is analysed with alarm, especially when previously your celebrity status may have invited only praise not criticism.'[37]

There would be very few CEOs of public companies who ever get an untroubled, glorious run that attracts no criticism. Sometimes an individual's timing can be immaculate but usually events — some within your control, some outside it — conspire to mean the journey of a company, and accordingly its CEO, has ups and downs. So you do have to develop an inner resilience that enables you just to carry on with whatever is in front of you, regardless of what the spectators in the stands are saying. However, the essence of what Bill wrote is very true.

I received a lot of support from all manner of people when John and I split up and a lot less support when I was part of the media furore around the regulation of Telecom. I think the different reactions were explained by the fact that most of us at some stage in our lives have major setbacks in relationships, so we know what it feels like, but very few people are subject to constant scrutiny in the media. I counted no less than eight opinion pieces in the May–June 2006 period blaming me, at least in part, for Telecom's fall from grace, and saying it was time for me to go.

It had been a dreadful period in my life, especially being single and having no one at home to support me. One day I had gone to Margaret Doucas's house and burst into tears. Chris Woodwiss had also been the most wonderful support at this time. Except for my very close friends I had felt very alone, perhaps the first time as CEO that I had felt this way. Sometimes one positive email in a day had made all the difference, and I got many of those from Telecom staff. I think most people are busy getting on with their own lives and don't notice one or two isolated pieces of criticism about public figures in the media, but when someone is at the centre of a media storm that goes on for days or weeks it does register in the public consciousness. When it's you being talked about or written about, it cuts to the very bone and you lose all sense of perspective and sometimes good judgement about how to handle the situation.

I've observed that people at the centre of a media furore usually choose flight, opting for saying little or nothing as the best way to have the story blow over and the news to move on to something else. Sometimes this works, although in a leadership position it's very easy for this to be portrayed as cowardly behaviour or ineffective leadership. A minority of people don't choose flight, they choose fight, and come out swinging in the media themselves. Occasionally this can work but it's very easy for this behaviour to be seen as aggressive or unworthy of whatever position the person holds, and it's particularly difficult for a woman to carry this off effectively as it goes against the grain of what's acceptable female behaviour.

By and large, I think New Zealand has a very good news media. In my experience, Kiwi journalists are decent people going about their job writing things as they see them. But as Karyn Scherer, a very experienced and insightful journalist at the *Herald* who's been written about herself a few times, observed to me recently, it's a salutary lesson for all journalists to occasionally be on the other end of the microphone or dictaphone and understand how it feels to be worried about what is going to be written about them.

Two of the most interesting and entertaining journalists writing in the New Zealand media today, Paul Holmes and Bill Ralston, always go to the heart of the subjects they are talking about but are very rarely unkind about people. I wonder whether their own experience of having been written about or spoken about, at times critically, by their peers has something to do with that.

New Zealand is a small country and we must all live together, yet we're often harder on our own people than those who come to our shores for a few years and then leave. I guess it's part of our tall poppy syndrome.

After I left Telecom I missed my team terribly. The executive team gave me a photo of themselves raising a glass to me as a leaving gift and I kept it in my home office for many months, but every time I looked at it I felt unbearably sad and eventually put it away for many months until I could look at it without getting upset.

I spent most of those first few post-Telecom months overseas avoiding winter in New Zealand, although I did come back a couple of times, when both Waikato and Victoria universities honoured me with alumni awards. My mum, Marion, was delighted to accompany me to both award ceremonies and my sister Yvonne was also able to join us at the Waikato event. When I came back for good in late spring, the weather was beautiful and I wandered around trying to work out whether Wellington weather had always been so good or whether I'd just been so busy I'd never noticed.

But I also felt at a complete loss. I was so used to a very structured life with lots of support on the basics of life and organisation, including office support and diary support. I'd always been so goal-oriented and so focused, but now I didn't know what I wanted to do next or where I wanted to do it. Some days I felt like I'd died, but of course I was still alive, it's just that nothing was as it had been. I did something

I never thought I'd do and went to see a counsellor. I only had a few sessions but I did find it quite useful in terms of getting unstuck.

The demands and challenges that must be met to attain a CEO role are insignificant compared with the mental and emotional stamina of staying in the position. It had taken almost all of me for 20 years to get there, and almost all of me for nearly eight years to stay there. I had had no idea how much I needed a rest and a change of pace.

I enjoyed a glorious summer in New Zealand. According to my father, it was a pleasure to spend time with me at the beach without my cellphone constantly ringing. I had a wonderfully relaxed time, full of friends and food and no stress. From the day I left Telecom I was able to indulge in my preferred nine hours' sleep a night — not a luxury any CEO gets — and little by little I began to savour the flexibility and peace of my new life.

I really didn't know what I wanted to do next. I had a hankering to do something entrepreneurial and had explored one or two opportunities in the United States, but ultimately they hadn't seemed quite right. I was pretty sure I didn't want to do anything in telecommunications, even apart from the fact that I'd signed a restraint of trade agreement.

I'd gone overseas with half a mind to living abroad, but come back to New Zealand and fallen in love with it all over again. I wanted to continue to have the sort of life I'd had — a life based in New Zealand, but with plenty of opportunities to spend time overseas in countries that I enjoyed, such as America and Australia.

Early in the summer, Margaret Doucas, who has been involved in animal welfare for most of her life, told me about the Wellington SPCA's $6 million project to create a new animal care centre. I went with her to look at the existing premises and was shocked at how inadequate they were. Then I went to see the intended new premises, in Wellington's old Fever Hospital, originally used to house tuberculosis and scarlet fever patients. Sitting on a superb site high on Mt Victoria at the edge of the Town Belt, it had been used until the 1980s for geriatric purposes and the exterior had been renovated by the city council. I believed that we must be able to do better for our animals than the existing cramped shelter and wanted to do everything I could to make the project happen, so I started out calling everybody I thought might be interested in helping and we organised a fundraising dinner for April. Margaret and I spent time with people who we identified might want to help in a substantial way, showing them around and talking about the project, and on the night we raised over $1 million in pledges from people who committed to sponsor different areas of the centre or to otherwise give donations. I embarked on this and worked hard for three months with no thought of anything other than the project itself, but I ended up getting so much out of it. I had given money to the SPCA for years, but it was a real pleasure to do something in a more practical, committed way.

Despite my enjoyment of this project, I had good days and bad days during this period. Sometimes I felt quite flat because I was struggling to envisage what future I wanted to create. Some people, after working hard in one direction for a long time, take time out and discover they have a talent for something they never realised, or a passion for art or something like that. In those first nine months I didn't discover any long-lost talents or passions I didn't realise I had, and while I did enjoy doing more of the things that I had previously done, such as riding my horse, I didn't want to make a profession of it.

The week after our successful fundraising dinner Judy Weir, then CEO of the Wellington SPCA, and I took prospective donors up to the old Fever Hospital to show them around. We were met by the caretaker employed by the council, whose role would no longer be required once the SPCA moved in. He acted very aggressively towards us. A couple of days later I got a call from a senior staff member at the council saying that the caretaker had shown up at the council offices in a very agitated state and they had had to call the armed offenders squad to take him away! They served him with a trespass notice saying that he must not go within 100 metres of either me or the mayor, Kerry Prendergast, about whom he had also made threatening comments. We were asked not to go to the Fever Hospital until further notice.

So that was the end of those fundraising efforts for the time being. I did have a chuckle, though, about the irony of being a high-profile CEO for nearly eight years and never once feeling unsafe or physically threatened, then having someone threatening to physically harm me following a few months doing voluntary work for the SPCA!

Unfortunately after Judy Weir left the SPCA at the end of 2008, the conversion of the old Fever Hospital into a new animal care centre appeared to no longer be effectively managed and by August 2009 the project costs had blown out to $9 million. Craig Shepherd, who was an SPCA board member and long-time supporter, raised legitimate concerns about the cost overruns with the project and questioned how it would be funded. After raising concerns about this and other matters he was formally censured by a majority decision of the board on a motion moved by the chair, Simon Meikle. This led to major ructions within the board, with three board members ultimately resigning, including Craig and Margaret.

When it was obvious that the project costs had blown out, I was willing to join the board to help specifically with the project. The chair made it clear that the majority of the board did not want me to join and stated that they could replace my experience, donations and donor contacts.

Naturally I was hurt but, more to the point, I couldn't see how this was in the best interests of the animals or Wellington in general. I considered it incredible that at the same time as the SPCA was calling for volunteers to stand on windy street corners for its annual appeal, the majority of the board had been instrumental in destroying the enthusiasm and commitment of three of its largest individual donors (myself, Margaret and Craig Shepherd). And this from an organisation that receives no government or direct local body funding and stands or falls on donations of its members and supporters.

The SPCA is a member-based society and I still believe it is a fantastic cause. I admire the work the SPCA staff and volunteers do.

So it was with great sadness that I felt I had no choice but to write to the board and let them know that while I would continue to sponsor animals at the existing shelter, as I had done for the past 20 years, I could not, in good conscience, continue to promote the campaign for the new animal care centre when I no longer had confidence that it was a viable project, or in the judgement of the board. Not surprisingly, this all came to a head shortly afterwards at the AGM, where a motion of no confidence in the existing board was passed. The following week the board met with three new members and it was announced that the project would be reviewed with a view to bringing it into line with earlier cost estimates.

Just as you can find goodness anywhere, you can find ego and tactics used to suppress dissent anywhere too. It was a big learning curve for me that inside a charity like this you could find people in leadership positions who, in my view, were displaying ego-driven, bullying tactics and behaving in a way that was anything but charitable.

During 2008 I was approached about a few roles overseas, both in the IT sector and in other areas that interested me but in which I had no previous work experience. I was flown to Asia to meet with a CEO in a different industry who was looking for a successor, and I set up opportunities myself through mutual colleagues to meet with CEOs of industries I was interested in. But ultimately none of this went anywhere. I wasn't clear enough in my own mind about what I would and would not do. All my life up until this point I had a really, really clear and strong career direction. It seemed to have left me, which has given me more empathy for those people who struggle to find vocational fulfilment, something that I'd always taken for granted.

Shortly after the SPCA fundraising dinner I went down to Queenstown for a week with John. We were very connected again as friends and of course he knew me very well and has always given me good advice. He thought I needed to do something that incorporated more of my feminine side.

I made plans to go to the United States in June to explore bringing great New Zealand fashion designers such as Trelise Cooper to California. I focused on Carmel-by-the-Sea, on the Monterey Peninsula and adjacent to Pebble Beach, the world-famous golf course. Salinas, the area referred to in John Steinbeck's *The Grapes of Wrath*, is close by. It is a very fertile area, the fruit and vegetable bowl of the United States, leading out to the magnificent, rugged coastline of Big Sur. Carmel itself is cute as a button. Undertaking any development there is a planning nightmare, which is why the place has kept its charm. You won't find a Starbucks, you won't find a high-rise. Everybody moves at a leisurely pace. There are inns rather than hotels. It is a very special place. And it's only two hours south of San Francisco, one of the coolest cities in the world.

The Monterey Peninsula is a very affluent part of the United States and many wealthy people have second homes in that area. Whenever I went there and wore Trelise Cooper, my favourite New Zealand designer, I was always complimented on my clothes. The bright colours and gaiety of her clothes suit the local vibe and sunny climate.

On one post-Telecom visit I was introduced by a friend of a friend to Sinda Mandurrago. She was a trained accountant managing her father's construction company, but she longed to do something more creative. I met her on two separate trips to ascertain whether we could successfully start a business together in this area, showcasing New Zealand clothing designers and particularly Trelise. Both curvy, we had a vision of a place that would feel like Trelise's stores in Auckland — a celebration of being a woman, whatever shape and size.

As an aside, I wear almost exclusively New Zealand designers. I do have a soft spot for shoe shopping overseas, but I am invariably disappointed when I purchase clothes outside New Zealand. My favourite designers are Adrienne Winkelmann for formal corporate wear and evening wear, and Trelise Cooper for day wear, whatever the situation, especially her gorgeous skirts and structured yet contemporary jackets and coats. I also have some treasured pieces from Liz Mitchell and Tanya Carlson, and over the last couple of years I have become quite a fan of some of the younger designers who are working with merino wool, such as Miranda Brown. When it's summer and I want to feel like I'm not really in my forties, I sometimes pull on one of Kate Sylvester's cool tops and shortish skirts. But Trelise is my all-time favourite: the beauty of the fabrics, the way the colours 'pop', the way the clothes feel on your body and the inspiring message sewn into every garment . . . I love them!

In February 2009 Sinda and I opened our store in Carmel, Charlotte Grace. Of course, our timing wasn't the greatest; between conceiving the idea and designing the store — which had a gorgeous, sumptuous feel but was welcoming at the same time — and its opening, shoppers in the United States stopped spending. Nevertheless customers have been so overjoyed at finding beautiful clothes at something other than wafer-thin US sizes that they sometimes hug Sinda! Trelise herself came across for our opening and organised a fashion parade — she has been a very generous supporter.

Chapter nineteen

off the sheep's back

The week in April 2008 that I was in Queenstown with John, I had a call from Craig Norgate, chairman of PGG Wrightson. (We had met when I was CEO of Telecom and he was CEO of Fonterra.) It may have been something about being in a South Island high-country setting, but I was intrigued about the picture he painted, of a product that should be a marketer's dream, which New Zealand produces in large quantities and in great quality, but which was languishing — an industry on the brink of collapse. He was talking about the wool used for carpets and interiors (called strong wool in agricultural circles). Like many Kiwis I really love wearing Icebreaker clothes and had admired the repositioning of merino wool, no longer seen as that scratchy thing you would never wear next to your skin but turned into a fantastic story linking environmental sustainability, comfort and fashion. I couldn't see why that couldn't be done for strong wool for carpets and other products as well. Here, finally, was the interesting but flexible sort of role I'd been looking for.

I met with several farmers, including Brian Lochore (a long-time farmer famous in New Zealand for his exploits as an All Black in the 1970s) who had previously had a crack at trying to do something about this many years before and was willing to give it another go, and John Perriam, owner of Bendigo Station and 'father' of both New Zealand Merino and of course the world's most famous sheep, Shrek. Brian was on the Wool Grower Holdings board and John was asked by WGH to go on the new Wool Partners board, which was now seeking a chair. I became quite hooked on the challenge.

In July 2008, when I came back to New Zealand from Carmel, we announced the formation of Wool Partners International, set up to be 50 per cent owned by the farmer cooperative Wool Grower Holdings and 50 per cent by PGG Wrightson. Wool, which used to be half of a sheep farmer's income, had fallen to less than 10 per cent and in many cases the amount farmers received for their wool barely covered the cost of shearing. Our goal is to unite growers, consolidate the clip and innovate in the market. What needs to happen in wool, and is now happening, parallels what is starting to happen in the meat industry, only in meat's case prices have gone up and down, whereas in wool prices have only gone one way. Twenty years ago manufacturers paid $6 a kilo for wool — now they pay less than $3. Yet those same manufacturers are selling their carpets for much higher prices than they did 20 years ago.

A whole generation of consumers overseas has grown up without being told about the benefits of wool, so that today less than 3 per cent of carpets sold in the United States are made of wool. In New Zealand around 70 per cent of carpets sold are wool or predominantly wool based, but even so I don't think we do enough to celebrate what a wonderful product it is.

And it is so in keeping with the times. Sheep need to be shorn for animal welfare reasons, and once they're shorn, they get up and they run around back outside. They aren't harmed by the process, and they just keep on growing wool.

I believe that consumers will increasingly place emphasis on values such as quality and craftsmanship and commitment to social and environmental responsibility. We are entering a decade when bling will be out. There will always be people who can afford luxury items and wool should always be able to command a price premium if it is positioned correctly. Authenticity will be 'the new black', and nothing is more authentic than being able to take wool from the back of a sheep in New Zealand, spin it into yarn in New Zealand, take the yarn straight to a manufacturing mill in the United States and then sell it in the US market, showing complete traceability all along the supply chain and linking the wool back to the actual farm that it came from.

It's taken me a while to start to work out what makes farmers tick. One thing that strikes me is that they tend to congregate in same-sex groups more than corporate types. What I mean by that is that organisations like Women in Dairying and Rural Women are very active and it's quite easy to speak to groups of women who are involved on farms. I have found farmers to be practical, direct, very hospitable, genuinely passionate about what they do, and good fun to be with. They also tell more 'blue' jokes than would ever be considered acceptable in a corporate environment!

The first presentation that I did to farmers was about 45 minutes long. After it, one of the farmers in the room came up to me and said, 'Theresa, that was about the right length, but don't make it any longer, because farmers aren't the sort of people who can sit still for an hour and listen to a person. If we could do that then we probably wouldn't have chosen to be farmers!'

There are times when trying to mobilise them feels like mustering sheep down from the high country. I do miss the positional power of being able to organise as I see fit. There is a powerful incentive in a corporate environment for people to line up behind their boss or, if they don't like the direction of the organisation, to leave. With agriculture, the backbone of New Zealand, you're dealing with a large number of autonomous commercial units, from family farms to farmer cooperatives, publicly listed companies and large private companies. Mixed motivations, on top of the constantly changing environment — whether it's exchange rates, prices of the products, other market signals, or just the weather — all combine to make matters quite complex.

As are the huge land-tenure issues in the high country. I hadn't long been appointed chair of Wool Partners when I came across Roberta McIntyre's history of the South Island high country, *Whose High Country?*[38] In it she neatly describes the tension since the mid-twentieth century between the pastoral industry in the South Island high country and the increasing challenge by urban dwellers who see the land as part of their heritage and expect to be able to access it pretty much at will.

Historically, high-country sheep farmers had very long-term leases of the land from the government, often in perpetuity. In 1998 the then National government invited leaseholders to commence negotiations with the Crown to determine which parts of their property might change from being a pastoral lease to freehold, and which parts from pastoral lease to Crown ownership. The basic idea was that land of conservation and public access value would be returned to the public estate in return for the lessee being allowed to freehold some land of productive value.

Conceptually this was hard to argue with. You've got a willing buyer and a willing seller, and the voluntary tenure-review process was essentially a swap, with any difference paid in cash. The leaseholders negotiated freeholding parts of their property that were suitable for sustainable commercial production in exchange for handing over other parts to the conservation estate, or sometimes to a special lease, with grazing under supervision.

In 1999 the Labour Party made a campaign promise to improve public access to the countryside. Over the next few years, with Labour in power, more and more tension built up around the tenure-review process. In May 2007 high-country sheep farmers were notified that rents on the remaining Crown pastoral leases would be hugely increased, because of the premium in the marketplace for community values such as location, landscapes and views, and the pressure on land for development. Not surprisingly, farmers were outraged and saw it as a plan to force them off their land.

By 2009 the Department of Conservation had managed to acquire around half of the total South Island high country for the DOC estate through tenure review. The most common land practice under DOC's management appears to be to allow nature to take its course!

This taking back of high-country land by DOC on behalf of the Crown has largely gone unnoticed by the rest of us — after all, there are only a few hundred high-country sheep farmers and there's now a generation of New Zealanders who have no link back to our farming roots and have never been on a farm. This is despite the fact that once you drive south out of Auckland, it's obvious that we are nothing but one big farm! But appropriation is appropriation, whether it's high-country sheep farmers' long-term leasehold land or money from Telecom shareholders. Something being popular, or being driven by a noble cause, does not necessarily make it right.

This tension between the then government's policies and high-country farmers led to Minaret Station in Wanaka taking a case against the Crown to the Land Valuation Tribunal. In July 2009, five years after the Crown submitted its first valuation as part of the rent review of Minaret Station, the tribunal released its decision, finding in favour of the farmers. The fundamental issue was whether 'amenity values' should be included within the value of the land exclusive of improvements (LEI).

The tribunal ascertained that there were two types of amenity values in the context of the case. The first type is extrinsic to the property and includes roads, infrastructure and community services, and there is no issue that this type of amenity value forms part of the LEI value. The second type of amenity value is intrinsic and includes views and proximity of features such as lakes, rivers and mountains — intangible benefits. It was this type of amenity value that was disputed between the Crown and Minaret. The Crown argued that intrinsic amenity values should be included in the rental value LEI. Minaret argued that they should not, because their effect produces a rent at odds with the context and principles of the legislation that governs a pastoral lease and the actual terms of the lease that strictly confine the runholder to a limited, grazing-only regime. In short, the Land Valuation Tribunal ruled that the Crown should not have added the value of lake and mountain views into the formula used to calculate the rents of pastoral farms.

As a result of the decision, the rent on Minaret Station will increase by 400 per cent from the previous rental set 11 years previously, from $4800 per annum to $20,000 per annum. But this is one-sixth the rent proposed by the Crown of $105,600 per annum.

While the case itself was specific to Minaret, the objective was to pursue a test case so that the result could be carried across all pastoral leases. Not surprisingly, it was greeted with huge relief by farmers. As Minaret's owner Jonathan Wallis, chairman of the High Country Accord representing lessees, said in a media release: 'To many farmers, the rents set by the Crown exceeded the gross income from the farm.'

In late July 2009, the new National government announced a change in policy on tenure review, the main changes being a move towards more use of covenants rather than Crown ownerships and dropping the lakeside policy, introduced in June 2007 by the Labour government, that withdrew funding for tenure review for any properties adjoining or within 5 kilometres of and visible from identified lakes. This policy had been aimed at targeting the creep of housing around New Zealand's beautiful southern lakes. Jonathan Wallis has pointed out that the Queenstown Lakes District Council, whose jurisdiction covers several of the lakes in question, has already introduced stringent planning rules covering lakeside development.

This is a vexed and complex subject, and it highlights the growing disconnect between urban and rural New Zealand. New Zealand is a country that was born off the sheep's back. We romanticise notions of the high country and yet a whole generation of New Zealanders now barely has any connection with a working farm. Agricultural products make up two-thirds of our exports, but farmers represent less than one-seventh of the population. This is not a helpful platform for the future of this country, which will continue to be based on our competitive advantage, which is that we grow primary products such as meat and wool efficiently.

One of the companies contracted to Wool Partners International, Glen Eden Wool Carpet, is based in Atlanta, the carpet-manufacturing centre of the United States. Occasionally people in the industry in New Zealand advance the idea that the finished product should be taken all the way from the sheep to carpet manufacture in New Zealand, rather than exporting raw products to have value added to them overseas. While it does make good sense to make use of facilities that are here, for example utilising our world-class spinners to export yarn rather than wool, it doesn't make sense to try to duplicate the huge capacity in carpet manufacture that already exists elsewhere in the world.

When we were in Atlanta late 2008, Wool Partners' chief executive Iain Abercrombie and I couldn't believe the beauty of the carpets some of these American manufacturers were producing. At Glen Eden there was one particularly gorgeous rug, custom designed for an apartment complex in Florida, that was so beautiful and tactile I couldn't stop looking at it and touching it. Similarly, a few days later in the New Jersey warehouse of Nourison, another high-end carpet manufacturer, we were amazed at how magnificent carpet after carpet was, all made either entirely or mostly from New Zealand wool, superior to anything I have seen in New Zealand.

At one of a series of meetings with farmers in April 2009, a farmer in Wanganui remarked to me that 'our rugged individualism is sending us broke'. At another of the same series of meetings, a long-time farmer stood up at a gathering south of Auckland and said to the 50 or so farmers in the room that as farmers, they were partly to blame for the situation they found themselves in. No one in the room disagreed, although there was a little bit of squirming in seats.

Most of the damage to the New Zealand wool industry has been

outside New Zealand's control in terms of the rise of the synthetic
carpet industry. But some of it is self-inflicted. We can be our own
worst enemies. Around the time the Wool Board was being gradually
disembowelled, the McKinsey Report of 2000 recommended that
commercial marketing organisations be established to replace the Wool
Board, to promote both fine wools and strong wools. This occurred
with fine wools but not with strong wools until nearly a decade later,
when Wool Partners was established. Contrast the fortunes of merino
over the last decade with the fortunes of strong wool . . .

I was totally unprepared for the reaction when Wool Partners
was formed in July 2008. The New Zealand Council of Wool
Exporters put out a media release calling Wool Partners a catalyst
for catastrophe. In my opinion, the only catastrophe in the industry
is what's happened for farmers over the last 20 years! The price of
strong wool has gone only one way — down.

The governor of the Reserve Bank, Alan Bollard, told me that the
price fall from the 1950s until now is the longest-running one-way
price series of any commodity of any industry in the world that he's
ever seen.

Throughout the last 18 months, Iain Abercrombie and I have been
horrified at the poor behaviours endemic in this industry: the lack of
ethics, the misinformation regularly supplied to farmers. It would not
be tolerated in any other setting. And we scratch our heads about why
this industry seems as if it has been left behind in the dark ages. I have
so much empathy for farmers who, faced with this, should logically
have given up long ago. And of course many have — they've gone to
dairy or simply grown grass to support the dairy industry. But most
sheep farmers still passionately care about the quality of their wool and
continue to do so even though there's no economic reward for that.

Anyone taking on a leadership position in this industry opens
themselves up to a level of vitriol and personal attack from participants
in the industry that I've never seen in any other situation. Mike
Petersen, the indefatigable and hardworking chairman of Meat &
Wool New Zealand, is regularly the target of attacks from people

preserving their own narrow self-interest who are unable to look at things from either the perspective of the farmers or the perspective of the customers, or the country as a whole. It wouldn't be so bad if they were honest about their agenda, but many times they are not.

But it's not just the industry. It's collectively all of us who caused this situation to be this bad and who have it within our power to do something about it. If you care about the sustainability of the planet, buy wool. There is no way to compare the environmental effects of wool with synthetic carpet produced from oil. The next time that oil goes to US$150 a barrel, and I believe it will, we cannot have a situation where we have a generation who know so little about wool that this does nothing to increase the demand for wool carpets. Wear wool, buy wool.

I was horrified recently to find out that 100 per cent polyester, non-biodegradable, non-recyclable imported fabric that emits toxins into the atmosphere during wear can actually achieve the Environmental Choice NZ (ECNZ) accreditation standard, whereas textiles made from wool grown from the backs of New Zealand sheep, spun in Lower Hutt and woven in Auckland, cannot. New Zealand company Inter-Weave has been trying for two years to get some traction on this matter. They recently used words to me such as 'utter despair and frustration' after being told by a Wellington architect that one of their New Zealand wool fabrics would not be put forward for a new government department building fit-out because it was too hard to specify. The architects were going for a green-star rating for the building and this wool fabric would not meet that criteria.

ECNZ, the standard-setting organisation, was established several years ago by the government. As a New Zealander I'm speechless about this situation, when wool growers are such an integral part of our economy and need our support. And given all the wonderful attributes of wool — resistance to flammability, its effects on purifying indoor air quality, extreme longevity and biodegradability — I can't believe that it doesn't even meet the so-called green building code in our own country.

Under ECNZ's current specification, it seems the New Zealand environmental choice label is attainable for imported virgin acrylic, nylon and polyester fabrics, as well as 100 per cent recycled polyester PET. But recycled content does not guarantee a minimal impact on the environment. PET contains hazardous substances such as antimony, arsenic, chromium, formaldehyde, volatile organic compounds (VOCs), cobalt, zinc, plasticisers and other questionable substances. PET textiles are manufactured overseas using the waste of the producing country and will ultimately end up in New Zealand landfills, where they will remain for centuries. Wool products can be reused and will slowly biodegrade, releasing valuable nutrients into the soil. Synthetic textiles are manufactured from finite, non-renewable resources such as petroleum, whereas wool is a locally produced, rapidly renewable and sustainable resource.

When I was simply an observer of the agricultural sector and understood little of it, I had admired Craig Norgate for his role in setting up Fonterra. Now that I was inside the industry looking out, my admiration increased further, as I understood more about the highly delicate balance between farmer control, commercial interests and the disciplines they force in an organisation compared with the traditional model of producer boards. Then all this is buffeted by global demand and supply issues for agricultural products which are outside the control of New Zealand as a country, let alone individual farmers, and which have such a profound impact on our fortunes.

New Zealand stands for a little bit of paradise in the eyes of much of the rest of the world. We don't build on the romance of that idea nearly enough. We don't have a brand for New Zealand that pulls together our tourism efforts *and* our trade efforts. After decades, the meat companies are starting to move away from a commodity approach to selling meat in overseas markets to starting with what customers want. New Zealand Merino presented packaging featuring the concept of 'alpine lamb' at its 2009 conference. What a fantastic name and what a great way to market meat coming out of New Zealand!

This matters to New Zealand, because in many ways it is the story of New Zealand. If we cannot get a higher value for the things we do well, such as meat and wool, we will never fulfil our potential as a country.

the view from outside

In New Zealand we seem to want to treat all large companies as if they were state-owned enterprises, i.e. able to be dictated to by government and required to balance social and economic objectives. And with utilities there is an ever-present threat of regulation: governments can never leave well enough alone.

The Telecommunications Act had a thorough overhaul in 2001, and important additions were made in 2004. Then in 2006 a major overhaul, introducing unbundling and operational separation, was made to that legislation, barely five years old. Certainly it had not been long enough for the 2004 changes to show results.

This level of intervention is not a good fit with the long-term investment cycles involved in these industries. It's a bit like multiple marriages: by the time you're on your third marriage, repeating various patterns, surely you can figure out well, maybe it's not my partner. Maybe it's me. Maybe I'd have been better off if I'd just stuck with my first partner and worked things through . . .

Utility regulation is rather like that. The need for a country to balance on-time, adequate capacity in energy and telecommunications to support its citizens, coupled with the right incentives to invest in an uncertain future and the citizens' legitimate desire to pay a reasonable price for the services provided, make for an inherently unstable mix. Add to that New Zealand's short election cycle. Whatever the political regime, the country is constantly faced with making these trade-offs. I think we'd be better off sticking with the model and adapting it around the sides than lurching from one extreme to another. In the space of six years, telecommunications went from operating under a very light-handed regime on a world basis to very prescriptive, heavy-handed regulation.

One day in September 2009 I got a call from an Australian business journalist asking me what I thought of the Australian government's announcement about Telstra. Not being as clued in to telecommunications matters across the Tasman as I used to be, I didn't know what he was talking about. After logging onto my PC I realised why he thought it was so momentous. I could hardly believe that lightning had struck the same place twice: in eerie parallel with the New Zealand government's moves on Telecom three years earlier, there was the Rudd government reshaping the telecommunications landscape to Telstra's detriment in the most brutal way possible. Under federal legislation introduced that day, Telstra would be compelled to split its operations or face drastic curbs on its future growth. Australian Communications Minister Stephen Conroy vowed to ban Telstra from buying the wireless spectrum it needs to deliver new mobile phone services unless the company submitted to a voluntary plan to break up its business. Senator Conroy said his clear preference was for Telstra to submit a voluntary plan to structurally separate, which would be examined by the Australian Competition and Consumer Commission. This would be achieved by amending the Radio Communications Act 1992 to prevent Telstra from acquiring specified bands of spectrum to use for advanced wireless broadband services unless it complied with the government's intention. Telstra was also being asked to devise an acceptable plan to get rid of its existing HFC (hybrid coaxial cable) network and its half share of Foxtel.

I think these are the sort of stand-over tactics that wouldn't be out of place in a dictatorship, especially when you consider that there hadn't been significant analysis around the AU$43 billion price tag put on the national broadband network which was the Rudd government's election campaign promise.

'We're offering them a choice,'[39] Senator Conroy was reported as saying. 'If they want to purchase a new spectrum that will be necessary for the future wireless technology, then they need to divest a number of other platforms.' Not much of a choice when mobile is the company's most important and largest revenue driver! And this came when Australians had barely filed away their Telstra share purchases following the previous government's decision in 2006 to sell the final tranche of Telstra to investors.

According to industry commentators, the result is the kind of regulatory maze where Telstra will keep running into brick walls until it chooses the corridor that suits the government: a full structural separation, followed by an agreement to sell its assets into the national broadband network.[40] That's a pretty interesting response to the constructive approach to government of the new Telstra CEO, David Thodey, and chair, Catherine Livingstone (Don McGauchie had stepped down as chair earlier in the year and Sol Trujillo, the previous CEO, had returned to the United States).

According to Conroy, the Australian government wants Telstra to structurally separate on a voluntary and cooperative basis. Well, as voluntary as it can be with a loaded gun at its head, anyway! If Telstra doesn't agree to do that the government will legislate to impose what they describe as a 'strong functional separation' on Telstra, under which it will be required to conduct its network operations and wholesale functions at arm's length from the rest of the company and provide equivalent price and non-price terms (such as service timeframes) to its retail business and non-Telstra wholesale customers — in addition to being banned from acquiring additional spectrum for its mobile network.

This puts the Telstra board in a terribly invidious position where they have to choose between the best of two bad outcomes for shareholders. Incredibly though, apparently the minister talked that up as well, reportedly saying that Telstra investors were the cause of recent falls in the company's share price, through their pessimistic public commentary.[41] Telstra's share price fell as a result of the government's moves. Quite frankly, I'm surprised it didn't drop more. In New Zealand the Telecom share price underperformed the market during the broader rally in share prices over the nine months from April to December 2009, mainly because its earnings prospects are so bleak given the New Zealand government's moves through 2006 and 2007 to tie it up in knots. And now the situation is being repeated in Australia.

Investors have certainly been more outspoken in Australia than they were in New Zealand. What I find incredible is that these sorts of blunt government interventions just wouldn't be tolerated in other industry sectors, but there seems to be something about infrastructure in general and telecommunications in particular that means the populace in Australia and New Zealand accepts huge lurches in direction as simply the outcome of a change of government.

By October 2009 media were reporting that Telecom–government tensions were rising.[42] But of course the new 'make nice' regime in New Zealand wasn't getting much more traction than the one in Australia. In New Zealand, however, we are oh so much more polite about it! But at the end of the day it's our money as taxpayers they are using to go around the major telcos and duplicate infrastructure.

In terms of broadband, my own view is that both the New Zealand and Australian public would have been best served by the governments coming to an arrangement (a very transparent one), with Telecom in New Zealand and Telstra in Australia, with regard to rolling out higher speed broadband. If they can't bring themselves to do that then they should be authentic about the problem, which in a nutshell is that broadband is like roading: it is never going to generate enough of a payback for a commercial company in return for what is required across the length and breadth of the country.

In October 2009, New Zealand's Minister of Communications Stephen Joyce, in inviting applications from private partners wanting to create local fibre companies to enable faster broadband, said that the government was prepared to meet 90 to 100 per cent of the upfront cost of laying fibre-optic cables to streets in the 33 cities and towns covered by the scheme. The government still expected its investment of up to $1.5 billion to be at least matched by the private sector, but it would foot the entire bill if the fibre network became a white elephant and customers didn't take up services because the price was too high. The private partners would pay to connect individual homes and businesses to the network, buying out a proportion of the government's share in local fibre companies only as customers took up the service. Joyce was reported as saying that the financing model was designed to overcome any concerns private investors might have about the uncertain demand for fibre.[43] The uncertain demand for fibre? Joyce is being realistic in my opinion. Interesting, then, that so many comentators have positioned the demand for high-speed broadband as more akin to finding water for thirsty people waiting beside an empty well!

Marko, my astute former CFO, has always been a man of few words and I can well remember a very pithy email he sent around the team as all of the debate around broadband and regulation was unfolding in 2006, in which he predicted that the (poor) economics of broadband would eventually be obvious to all. Well, it's 2009 and they're becoming rather more clear.

As I said previously, broadband is the 'virtual' equivalent of roading — and not just in terms of investment. If the country is not well served by this essential infrastructure, then by all means change the model of how it is supplied. Governments have the right to do that. Renationalise Telecom/Telstra. Or come up with some other model. But be authentic and upfront about it. Don't blame a private-sector company (Telecom in New Zealand) for not acting in the public interest when the board and management team have a legal duty to their shareholders, not 'the 'public', and don't pretend to offer a 'choice' to a company over structural separation (Telstra in Australia) when they really have no choice at all.

And compensate those who are the current owners of the companies who are going to suffer if there is a fall in the value of the company directly arising from a change in the regulatory framework. In New Zealand, Maori forestry interests acquired under Treaty settlements are to be compensated for the forests' loss of value under the carbon emissions trading scheme. How is this different from compensating Telecom shareholders for the loss of value directly suffered from the introduction of a new telecommunications regime?

Chapter twenty-one

on being
a CEO

CEOs are the public face of many of these essential policy issues. What I enjoyed most about being CEO was being at the centre of the action and the constant variety that each day brought. I loved being at the centre of a team of competent, committed, strong people, all working together for the good of the company. I enjoyed seeing things that we'd thought about and planned come to pass and be successful. If I could rewind the tape, I'd do it all again in a heartbeat although, knowing what I know now, I'd do it a little differently.

(One thing I would have done differently, which is a small thing but potentially powerful, would have been to have Telecom executives pay for their own phone and internet, even though it would have been reimbursed. Because phone and internet were provided by the company it was very easy to have every new gadget and service going and to become somewhat disconnected from what customers would perceive as value for money, which would have become blindingly obvious if you yourself were paying for it. Of course, you can get that information from looking through reams of research, which I regularly did, but it's not the same.)

The job definitely came at a cost: the cost of my relationship, the cost of being out of balance as a person — only having time for people who were functionaries in my achievement-oriented universe. I switched off my 'feminine' side years ago in order to get to the top in a man's world, then I found some difficulty in switching it on again, although I've been told that I'm more relaxed and easier to be around now than I have been for years. I've certainly enjoyed being a free agent.

Still it wasn't just that job that made me so single-minded. If I'd been more talented and learned to ride earlier, I might have channelled my energies into being a competitive horsewoman. And I would have been just as focused and bordering on being obsessive about that. At the end of the day, you take yourself wherever you go!

The hardest thing I found about being CEO was constantly being judged. I had no problem being on top of the material on the issues but I found it very hard to deal with the relentlessness of being watched and dealing with people's different agendas, which drove them to take stances that might have nothing to do with what I'd meant. At times it was hard to avoid sounding defensive.

There was no such thing as a typical day, except that I always got up at 6am, did my swim training, had my hair done at a salon on the way to the office to deal with post-swimming 'pool hair', read and responded to emails when I got in, and generally never started meetings before 8.30. When I was first CEO I could count on not getting very many emails over a weekend, but by the time I left, email traffic had become a 24-hour, seven-day-a-week phenomenon.

When you're a CEO you're never not working. It doesn't matter whether you're at your desk, in transit somewhere or at home. For the last few years everybody has had a BlackBerry or similar PDA device that continually brings emails to you, no matter where you are or what you're doing. That's just part of the job.

A CEO never has a minute to spare. That is the truth of the matter. You're always working on intersecting cycles: the daily cycles of meetings, the weekly cycles of receiving reports — indicators on key numbers and other important information, the monthly cycles of getting full monthly data and preparing and reading board papers prior to board meetings, and the three-monthly cycles of reporting to the market and presenting to analysts. And then there are the media cycles that you are both generating or getting caught up in inadvertently, as part of other people's cycles, be they political, competitors or changing consumer tastes. At the end of the day it's about people interacting with people, all of you striving to do the best you can.

I've made lifelong friends in every work situation I've ever found myself in. You go through a range of emotions together, celebrating successes and achievements and supporting each other when things don't go so well. And you don't leave that behind at the end of a day or the end of a job. That camaraderie is one of the things that has made my business career to date so enjoyable.

I have also learnt from all the bosses I have had in my corporate life and from many of my colleagues. From my first boss, Murray Higgs at Fisher & Paykel, while I was still a business school student, I learnt to feel comfortable about being challenged by someone who was smarter than me — and knew a lot more about the subject matter. From Murray McKinnon, my boss at TVNZ, I discovered the sheer power of a manager who works so hard that you feel you need to work hard alongside them, and experienced the huge joy of working for a man who was not at all threatened by female managers who were not just strong and intelligent but quite lateral and spontaneous. Also at TVNZ I met Cindy Mitchener, which was the start of a life-long friendship. During our years working together there we were quite a dynamic duo, staking out the jobs that we thought needed to be done and writing our own position descriptions by broadening our roles as we went.

From Roger Oly, my boss at National Mutual, I learnt the power of praise and in particular the power of a handwritten note — the power of making an emotional connection with the people who work for you and support you. From Lindsay Pyne at the Bank of New Zealand, I learnt the power of being deeply challenged while simultaneously being given a lot of autonomy. Lindsay also taught me the strength and fun that come from being part of a powerful team. And from Roderick Deane, I learnt the power of disciplined processes, deep analysis and acceptance that everyone is different and executive diversity is to be valued.

As my CEO, and later as the chairman of the Telecom board, Roderick was good to me. He is a wonderful mentor to talented people in all walks of life and was always very encouraging. He gave me a huge break, promoting me from general manager – marketing to running the wider New Zealand business, and then was instrumental in my becoming CEO. I believe that my total focus on becoming CEO of a large company and my determination would have got me there eventually, but I absolutely have no doubt that his support got me there faster.

Wayne Boyd was good to me at the end of my time as CEO. A lesser man, on becoming chairman in the eye of such a storm, would have wanted to visibly stamp his leadership on the situation, fuelled by ego. The obvious way for a chairman to have done that would have been to have swapped out the CEO. Given that he was no doubt under pressure from some quarters to do just that, his decision to work quietly with the existing team in shaping the choices he made is testament to the person that he is.

These people were all mentors in one way or another. I also had a good external mentor during my Bank of New Zealand years in Dr Sharon Lord, an American who became the highest-ever ranked woman at the Pentagon. She lived in New Zealand for several years after she married Tom Burns, who was from Bell Atlantic and was the CEO of Telecom for just under a year before Roderick Deane. She consulted widely on women in management across Australia and New Zealand and was a very helpful sounding board in those times, helping me to navigate the pathway from middle to senior management. Over the years I have found many senior people, even very busy, committed ones, enjoy being sought out for the value of their experience and the wisdom that comes with it.

I have never had any formal CEO or executive coaching. In fact, I find the whole idea slightly bizarre, as most of the people who I've seen offering those services have never been in those roles themselves. I've always felt more comfortable talking to people who have trod a similar path themselves and who can therefore see a bigger picture, such as Kevin Roberts, who has long been a mentor of mine.

A big difference between being a senior executive, even one with a large team of thousands of people, and being the CEO is, of course, the public profile. But a second big difference is interacting with a board. I found every Telecom board meeting different. Most I enjoyed, a few I dreaded, occasionally I was bored. But I think I made a mistake of not interacting more with the whole board outside formal meetings. I think most first-time CEOs make the mistake of focusing on their relationship with the chair of the board because they see that as the natural extension of the relationship they've previously had with a boss in a corporate setting. You go from being, for example, a general manager reporting to a CEO, and now you're a CEO reporting to a chair.

I have seen every permutation of what happens with boards when trouble descends upon a company. I have seen boards, including the chair, turn on CEOs; I have seen chairs dump CEOs before the board could dump them; I've seen boards turn on CEOs and chairs together. I've also seen boards totally hang in together in bad situations. And now, being on the other side of the fence, I have more empathy for the position of board members, who come at things from a different perspective to that of a full-time executive who's living, sleeping, eating, breathing the company every minute of every day. On a board you can sometimes see when a CEO is not quite seeing the wood for the trees, or missing something that's happening in the wider world that's very relevant, because they're immersed in their own situation. But of course you also lack a lot of detail, and I believe a boardroom is a very poor place to make judgements about senior executives in particular. Roderick occasionally carried out surveys of the board to judge satisfaction with governance matters, including board–senior management interaction, and I was stunned when in one of these surveys the board indicated that they believed they could judge an executive's performance on the times they saw them in front of the board. But in a way that's what we all do — judge on that which we see.

I think CEOs make a mistake if they rely on the chair to manage the board. It is certainly true that it's the chair's role to manage the meeting, to focus it on the right issues in the right order, to set a standard of respect and to manage the mechanics around setting the CEO's performance targets and specific coaching. But nobody wants to feel that they're being managed, and the whole point of a board is to have a diversity and variety of experience and background that will lead to better overall decisions and outcomes. Sometimes that is not comfortable for the CEO.

Having both been on several different boards and a CEO, I can see that the basic tension is around the epicentre of power. Information flows in a company centre on the CEO, media attention centres on the CEO, and yet directors and therefore boards have strong legal duties to do what's in the best interests of the business. That may not necessarily be what management thinks is in the best interests of the business or indeed what's in management's *own* best interests.

Board composition is a subject that has been written about at length. One of the tensions within a board can occur around whether the members are thinking primarily of the company's interests or those of the individual stakeholders. I personally have never been part of a board where I thought that anything untoward was happening, but natural tensions do emerge. As Bob Jones once said to me, 'The theory of a public company board is very good, Theresa, but the practice can be awful.'

It's an interesting dynamic being a woman CEO managing an executive team which is largely male and, let's face it, most women CEOs are managing groups of men. You do need to be quite strong but I also found it was important to have a light touch. If a woman can stay balanced between being authoritative, which tends to be a male characteristic, and empathetic and communicative, which tend to be female characteristics, then the men she is working with can feel relaxed in her company, but it's not always an easy balance to strike. In my experience men in a corporate setting are more likely to share their vulnerabilities and worries and concerns and honest appraisals of a situation with a woman rather than another bloke. But the pressures on a CEO are such that you tend to get pushed into not having the time to tune into your empathetic side and end up being in authoritative mode most of the time.

I was treated as an equal by my male colleagues in the corporate world. That's what women want of course, but for me in a way it reinforced my being in a 'male' mode. This was not the case with my immediate team, however, where the relationships were much more nuanced and I felt able to be more my 'complete' self.

My executive team and I went away for occasional off-site meetings to increase relatedness within the team. Carefully constructed, I think these do work — at least they always have for me. I believe that the time we are living in now is all about authenticity, and that the most important thing a leader can be is authentic. When I was younger I thought leadership was largely about personality and determination and desire, and because I am an extrovert I tended to see leaders as more likely to be extroverts than quieter, more reflective types.

Over the years I've come to see that personality has very little to do with it. Leadership is about *character*; it's about courage and steadfastness, about not asking anyone to do anything you wouldn't be prepared to do yourself. It's about passion and belief in the goals of the organisation and the team that you are heading, an acknowledgement of everyone's effort to make the whole greater than the sum of the parts.

The other thing I enjoyed about being CEO was being able to

make a difference. When the Film Archive went into its new home in Wellington, I remember driving past it every day on the way home and feeling positive about enabling that to happen through the BNZ's sponsorship of it when I was head of marketing. Fifteen years after we helped set up the Kiwi Recovery programme, I am delighted that the BNZ is still supporting this effort to protect and preserve our national bird.

From my days at National Mutual presenting workshops to women on taking control of their financial affairs, through the many speeches I've given to groups of women, from schoolgirls to professional women — female accountants, female lawyers, female farmers — I have often received feedback that something I've said switched on a light bulb for them, which helped them wherever they were at the time. I feel proud of the work I did with colleagues in Media Women, an informal group of feminist women who worked in the media and at TVNZ 25 years ago, on the portrayal of women in advertising, raising consciousness of that issue in the media and among advertising agencies.

As part of my CEO's role I launched video conferencing between schools to support education in far-flung communities, worked with Starship Hospital to launch a medical diagnosis service for regional hospitals around New Zealand using broadband technology, and led the dawn ceremony on Takapuna Beach for the lighting up of the Southern Cross cable, enabling telecommunications capacity for New Zealand for the next decade.

Being a CEO is a bit like living the life of a high-performance athlete. You're on the go and you're travelling so much that you need to have strategies for managing your rest and getting enough sleep and exercise. You need a dedicated pit crew: a fantastic executive assistant who you can trust to be efficient and well organised and to make appropriate judgement calls, and a supportive home structure, however that is configured. Through all my years at Telecom I was lucky enough to have had one of the best executive assistants anywhere in Chris Woodwiss.

There's definitely something quite selfish and rather unbalanced about being a CEO. You can only maintain the necessary pace if people around you work almost equally hard to support you. But making these sacrifices is all worth it when you receive the adrenalin buzz of those moments when everything is in flow.

In my middle years as CEO, I often felt this way. I had recruited or promoted an outstanding team and although we were often under pressure, we had a lot of fun together. I used to read business books, having always been a voracious reader of many different genres, and distil them in an interesting way for the team.

By this time, I felt I had successfully achieved a culture change at Telecom. In a work environment, most people will adopt the prevailing culture of the situation they find themselves in. A certain proportion will try to act in a harmonious way in whatever situation they find themselves, and a minority will have a tendency to throw a pebble into the pond just to see what ripples it causes. By my middle years as CEO I felt we had achieved a very cohesive working environment. Effecting such a major change is a very enjoyable process for those who are part of it, although there are inevitably some casualties. I do believe that sometimes you need to refresh the gene pool. It's very difficult to see yourself as others see you once you've been in the same place for several years.

I felt fantastic about the culture I'd put together at the top of Telecom in my last four years as CEO. We had almost no turnover in the top 100 leaders and a real sense of working together across the company. That's one of the reasons why I could never have led the company in an environment of operational separation. I just don't believe in warring tribes. I think there are so many pressures on a company from outside that you cannot maximise outcomes for customers or shareholders if you have division internally, especially following a government-mandated division with someone else pulling the strings. That would have been a living hell for me.

While I was CEO I always felt highly supported by my team and respected by the board. People say it's lonely at the top, but I never felt lonely until the end. At that time those close to me were dealing with their own stress, confusion and dismay about the turn of events, and at times I felt isolated and unsupported.

The good times never last, of course. The world shifts on its axis, the product that was ahead of its time is now behind the game, the government changes, the policies for the sector are under review, a major shareholder enters or exits and has a different vision of the future . . . you never know what's going to happen next.

Succession planning is a key part of any CEO's role but many do not do it well because their egos do not allow them to think that *anyone* could do the job as well as them, or they go for a 'lite' version of themselves because they think only someone like them could do the job. I took succession planning seriously and over several years developed and nurtured two internal candidates who were quite capable of following me as CEO: Marko Bogoievski, the chief financial officer, and Simon Moutter, chief operating officer. However, as things turned out, when the then board chose a strategy of complete capitulation to the government, neither of them was suited to the job and neither of them wanted it then anyway.

Marko in particular advocated strongly for a full structural separation. He believed that operational separation, with all its inherent contradictions and hugely embedded costs that would add no value, was doomed to not deliver for either shareholders or customers. He felt it could only ever be a transitory model on the way to somewhere else, so you may as well get to the somewhere else straight away and have a chance of a clearly transparent method of delivery to customers. Recently he has commented publicly about this, saying, 'Operational separation is an unnatural, large market idea imported from the United Kingdom with zero analysis and will be exposed as an unstable and disappointing transitory regime in the New Zealand context.'[44]

Given that Telecom's profits have halved in two years under operational separation, I am surprised that line of logic hasn't surfaced more strongly yet with investors. Profits are profits. ANZ Bank in

New Zealand reported a profit of $1 billion and no one batted an eyelid. Telecom made profits around $800 million and it was seen as grand larceny. It can only be because people believe that those profits were unearned, the result of a windfall arising from the original public nature of the infrastructure — even though the company was privatised in 1990 and hundreds of millions of dollars were invested in the infrastructure every single year subsequent to that!

For a long time after I left Telecom, I beat myself up. What did we miss? What did *I* miss? How did Telecom suddenly become treated more like a political party than a business? And now that I'm long gone I, along with the rest of the country, wonder about the propriety of a company making half the annual profits it did a few years ago but paying its executives considerably higher salaries.

Since leaving Telecom, I have come to understand that I am too direct for my own good and some people are just not comfortable with that. But I like myself and I'm not about to change. I have also come to see in a very painful way that only those closely involved in a situation ever know the full story. Everyone is looking at it through their own filter or a partial lens. That doesn't stop spectators in the stands rushing to make a judgement — or me, for that matter, making judgements on other matters on which I have only a partial perspective. It seems humans are hard-wired to be able to take in only peripheral information about things that we are not closely connected with. We tend to filter out a lot of stuff and hear only 'the facts' that support the story we are already attached to in our own heads.

This explains why I cherish those people who have been around the block with me and why I don't make new friends as quickly as I used to. People can be a lot more complex and multi-layered than they appear and I feel I can only really get to know someone over many years of closely interacting with them.

Chapter twenty-two

where to for business?

It is an article of faith that competition in the market is good for business and the consumer because it sharpens everyone's act, drives down costs and propels innovation. No one wants a Soviet economy but in a tiny market like ours competition can come at a cost.

For example, it is inarguable that Fonterra has been good for dairy farmers and good for New Zealand. But a special Act of Parliament had to be passed to allow Fonterra to be created because by any normal measure it would have been seen as anti-competitive. Contrast the fortunes of dairy farmers since 2001 with what has happened to sheep and meat farmers, where there has been the complete opposite of the consolidation we've seen in dairy — fragmentation of production and marketing in meat and wool. The improving returns to dairy farmers and the poor returns to sheep farmers in the last decade speak for themselves.

A small country like New Zealand needs some global champions.

Fonterra is one such company. Telecom could have been such a company — and perhaps still could be — but the cry to castrate it and bring it down to a level playing field with the branch offices of overseas multinational firms such as Telstra and Vodafone became deafening.

New Zealanders have an in-built aversion to big companies. I believe it comes from our heritage of proud independence. My parents were from Britain, absolutely archetypal immigrants from the UK, looking to create the future rather than be stuck in a box arising from patterns of tradition or history or place of birth. Collectively we left England to escape to a place where Jack could indeed be as good as his master, because here the boundaries between them were much more fluid.

New Zealanders encourage entrepreneurialism up to a point. We encourage people who give two fingers to the boss and go off to start their own business. But once they move beyond having a nice car and nice home to having a holiday home, a very nice car, a boat and so on, then they start to be seen as 'the other'.

Business cannot ignore the fact that it is part of an interdependent society. Nor can Kiwis escape the fact that even their largest businesses are tiny — merely flotsam and jetsam in the ocean of global industries in which they operate.

My time leading Telecom New Zealand corresponded with a tipping point of our times: the move from an analogue to a digital world, in which the boundary between 'public goods' and 'private goods' shifted. This can be seen particularly in the digitisation of information, photography, film and music, which is challenging the notion of property rights and hence what resides in the private versus the public sphere. These days it is quite hard to find a CD store still in business as downloading of music over the internet has become so pervasive.

This has also led to a democratisation of the creative sphere. Now anyone can be an artist to quite a sophisticated level. The creation of films, music and photography has become cheaper, simpler and more accessible. Alongside this comes the democratisation of business and politics. The internet means anybody can be a trader, adviser or commentator.

At its core the internet is essentially anarchic, allowing us to communicate with millions of people. One person's view becomes just as important as the next person's, which means that the old patriarchal model of being told how or what to think has gone right out of the window.

At a recent series of Wool Partners workshops for farmers, I started out by asking whether there were any journalists present. A couple of days into the workshops I started reading blogs and stories in the rural media written by farmers who'd been at the meetings. I realised how ridiculous it was to ask whether there were any journalists present because every single farmer in the room could communicate and publish his views as soon as we'd finished the meeting.

On the internet there is no hierarchy, no absolute source of truth, no one answer. I don't know whether a growing sense of interconnectedness led to the development and huge growth of the internet or whether the internet itself has spurred that feeling of interconnectedness, but it has certainly been heightened. Connecting with your true tribe has never been easier and will get more so. The underlying basis of the tribe is changing, too: it's becoming less about locality and ancestry and more about shared values. The internet has helped to facilitate this.

Communities are now as likely to be based on common interests as they are on geographic locality. The 2008 US presidential election was more closely followed by people outside the United States than any other American election in my adult lifetime, at least partly because of that sense of global connectedness.

The global financial crisis has reinvigorated the G20, which brings together the developed and developing worlds, and moved it from being a finance ministers' meeting into a leaders' summit. Global financial imbalances caused the crisis, not simply a collapse in the sub-prime mortgage market. And this has brought to front and centre the question, what is the nature of sustainable growth?

As Shaun Carney, associate editor of the *The Age*, Melbourne, has noted, there are some signs that concerted action through the G20 might just have averted a near bottomless financial plunge. That sort of thing would have been unachievable even as recently as the early 1990s, when national economies all traded autonomously and global economic forces were often viewed as immutable.[45]

And as US President Barack Obama — the first internet-generation president of the United States — observed in his inaugural address to the United Nations in September 2009, 'those who used to chastise America for acting alone in the world cannot now stand by and wait for America to solve the world's problems alone. We have sought — in word and deed — a new era of engagement with the world. And now is the time for all of us to take our share of responsibility for a global response to global challenges.'

Co-creation is the energy of the next decade. Governments dictating to the populace, and businesses dictating to customers, will be completely out of step with the times. Yet understanding there has to be a better way doesn't necessarily mean it can be achieved unless a critical mass of leaders also get it. When I was in Washington in October 2009 for the third United States–New Zealand Council Forum, representing Wool Partners, several of Washington's top lobbyists told us that, unfortunately, gridlock in the American political system between the Republicans and the Democrats had never been worse.

I also believe that spiritual consciousness in the West is moving away from traditional Christian ideals and more towards an integrated spiritual philosophy that incorporates Eastern religious principles and practices. These include meditation and yoga, knowledge of the self arising out of studies in psychoanalysis, evolutionary biology and psychology, and increasing environmental consciousness.[46]

In countries such as New Zealand, environmental consciousness started out with activists who were mainly to the left side of the political spectrum, but in the United States I don't perceive there was ever quite such a dichotomy and now it's becoming mainstream. This is an opportunity for countries like New Zealand because our products can be marketed as environmentally conscious, but it is also a threat in the sense that it puts pressure on our farming practices, for example.

The implication of this is likely to be a new, slowly emerging, hybrid moral and ethical code in the West that is not directly linked to Christian capitalist traditions. Associated with this shift in spiritual consciousness will be a rebalancing away from 'male' principles and fixed ways of looking at things — i.e. 'If we could just get the world to look like this and stay like this, all our problems would be solved' — and solutions arising out of left or right political ideologies, such as 'I'm right and therefore you're an idiot', ultra-rationalism, ego, self-promotion and motivation through fear. There will be a move towards 'female' principles, including the concept of disequilibrium, i.e. all structures are unstable and impermanent. There will be consideration of multiple possibilities and holistic solutions, a focus on the integration of ideas, more compassion, and less inclination to look for solutions in material objects or institutions.

A friend noted to me recently that at the well-heeled primary school her son and daughter attend, come 3 o'clock there are around 10 fathers waiting to pick up their children. That same weekend a journalist wrote in one of the major Sunday papers about this phenomenon: 'The one my son goes running to across the field each day once that final bell rings is my husband.'[47] Evidence in Britain also suggests there are more dads waiting at the school gate. While there have always been some men who have temporarily or for many years been the primary caregiver for their children because their wife earned good money or the nature of their work meant they were able to work from home or more flexibly, I detect a stronger movement of fathers who are taking equal share in bringing up their children than ever before. It's like anything in life: when there's just one or two people doing it, it's easy to be marginalised.

But once it hits critical mass then you're looking at a societal trend. Fathers who are waiting at the gate at my friend's children's school are not fathers with lower income than their wives. In many cases they're men in their forties or fifties who have worked full time for 20 years, built financial security and now are no longer working at breakneck speed, partly because they want to have a meaningful, more involved role with their children rather than that being just the consequence of their occupation.

What we're seeing now among high net-worth individuals in New Zealand will become mirrored wider out into the middle class. This won't be the story for all alpha males of course, or indeed for the majority. But more and more men are going to choose to spend time hanging out with their kids. This will be the start of an era more inclusive of fathers and less judgemental about mothers, as mothering and fathering come closer together.

I also believe we're going to see a reassessment of the value of 'moral wisdom'. According to psychologist Barry Schwartz,[48] the West has experienced demoralisation in recent times, becoming too dependent on the use of specific rules and financial incentives to shape behaviour. We have relied too little on 'discretion with moral wisdom'. An increase in this will generate some of the momentum towards a new focus on moral conduct in an emerging new ethical code. The most significant and long-term effect of the world financial crisis is likely to be a weakening of trust in both business and the government, as the crisis arose due to a combination of market and government failure — namely central banks generating easy money while regulators failed to keep pace with financial innovation.

Lord Patten, the last British governor of Hong Kong and member of the House of Lords, who visited New Zealand at the end of 2008, told the following story to business leaders in Auckland: 'In 2007, a young banker explained to me how the mortgage of a single unemployed African-American woman in Alabama could be moved into a special investment vehicle which you could buy and sell at great profit from Frankfurt to Shanghai to London. I couldn't understand what he was talking about. The trouble is, as it turned out, neither could he.'[49]

The financial crisis has also heightened awareness of debt accumulation. Climate change has increased sensitivity to environmental issues and the concept of sustainability. The children of the hippie generation are now adults and are more attuned to green issues than their parents.

More generally, the combination of digitisation and changes in spiritual philosophy will see the expansion of the personal responsibility ethic. But of course some people will remain in the old paradigm and this is likely to increase tensions.

An individual's personal philosophy is likely to be more influential on their behaviour than their age, as has been the case in the past. 'Amortality' was a word coined in 2009 by Catherine Mayer in *Time* magazine to describe how increasing life expectancy and changing social patterns mean that the differences between the generations will narrow. 'The defining characteristic of amortality is to live in the same way, at the same pitch, doing and consuming the same things, from late teens right up till death.'

Because of this emphasis on personal philosophy, the most important attribute of the new business will be an emphasis on authenticity: products, services and business behaviours that embody a genuine, transparent, committed and consistent adherence to an explicit set of core values. These will include ideals of trust and honesty and are likely to also include a commitment to environmental sustainability and social responsibility.

Authentic business will ultimately be about the dissolution of ego of both producer and consumer. The producer will have a lower profile and will meet less overtly materialistic needs. Inauthentic business behaviours will completely run out of steam — things like sending out birthday cards that simply say 'Happy Birthday' printed on very expensive, heavyweight card with at most a handwritten 'Dear Theresa' from whatever is the name of the store, and pretty much any kind of telemarketing. Basic human courtesies will be used to reinforce this authenticity, e.g. the tradesperson who takes off his shoes before entering your home.

I believe the United States will pioneer a new social contract between business, government and consumers/taxpayers. There may be a move away from contracting out services and manufacturing, as this potentially runs against authenticity. Some of what is today contracted out will come back inside firms, and in other cases the relationship between parties will be adapted to more a form of collaboration. There will be a continuing focus on collaborative product development, especially where it taps into the diversity of human creativity. The iPhone is a good example of how third parties can contribute to organic product development, with Apple releasing a set of codes that allowed third-party applications to be developed very easily.

In economies centred on entrepreneurship and innovation, and especially in the United States, opportunities in business renewal tend to arise out of crises. Microsoft and Intel both arose out of the 1970s oil crisis, when US manufacturing was in a mess. Google arose in the aftermath of the dotcom bust. The financial crisis and the end of the Bush neo-conservative foreign relations period has opened a door to a new political and business environment. Authentic business will be an important aspect of this new environment, including environmentally sustainable agriculture, organic farming and horticulture where there is some kind of authentication process establishing traceability of origin.

This trend is one of the reasons that I am passionate about championing wool, and New Zealand wool in particular. It is the most sustainable, authentic product imaginable. The sheep are shorn, then they get up and run off into the paddock, where they eat the grass and grow more wool. Science has yet to develop a product as fantastic as nature has produced. The success of New Zealand Merino, working with manufacturers who value sustainable farming practices, outdoor activity, luxury and traceability, has demonstrated the way of the future.

I believe there will be an increasing focus on statements of simple core values that are overtly non-financial. There will be a rejection of self-promotion or overt displays of ego, and a move away from bling for bling's sake towards more design-conscious products. 'Excess is out and prudence is in' screamed the headlines in *Women's Wear*

Daily on October 19, 2009. A year after financial markets had melted down, in the luxury goods industry the penny was starting to drop that conspicuous consumption appeared to be on the wane. In art there will be a return to the 'truth in beauty' ideals of a romantic age, and products that are committed to strong aesthetics will have considerable status.

We will see, and are already seeing, the rise of the oily rag ethos, in which making do becomes fashionable again. This will generate businesses that support that ethos, e.g. firms that refurbish second-hand goods, especially retro products like 1970s watches, stereos and film cameras; companies that provide generic ingredients for day-to-day use such as bulk foods and cleaners; businesses that offer simple, environmentally friendly, long-lasting products such as glass containers, wool clothing and sewn products; and business models like pre-pay systems, representing a move away from borrowing money to buy things. My generation of baby boomers was encouraged by parents, brought up during a war, to believe in a culture of working hard to achieve financial security. Our children's generation started out with high expectations of an upwardly beneficial financial curve, but aren't necessarily prepared to work as hard for it as we were. However, many of them have found themselves learning to make do by default, and being quite good at it.

In April 2009 the *New Zealand Herald* reported that, 'The trend towards thrift will not disappear when the economy picks up. For one thing, those banks left standing will be far more parsimonious with consumer credit. For another, many people will still be intent on rebuilding their nest eggs. Now many people no longer seem consumed by the desire to consume. Instead, they are planning to live within their means and there has been a backlash against bling. Some firms are already trying to capitalise on this new mood. Sears recently revived a saving plan it used many years ago known as the "lay away" programme, under which the consumer can make a down payment on an item that is being held for him or her for a fixed period, while he saves the rest of the cash needed to buy it.'[50]

Philanthropy will be more of a focus. The rise of modern capitalism in the nineteenth century initiated the age of 'heroic materialism' but from early on this was moderated by ideals of compassion and kindness. Philanthropy was a strong aspect of business in the late nineteenth and early twentieth centuries — think of Carnegie, Rockefeller, Getty. While Warren Buffett and Bill and Melinda Gates have become the new high-profile philanthropists, much smaller-scale philanthropy will become more commonplace. GDP will increasingly be seen as a less important indicator of success as other measures, including wellbeing. Nicolas Sarkozy has recently suggested introducing this concept of measuring progress in France.

There will be some backlash against digitisation, with greater discernment of the benefits of analogue, whether that's vinyl records, film cameras like the old Box Brownie, or hand-made products. This will be supported by 1970s and '80s culture, when analogue was at its peak, becoming trendy again.

A recent study of young adult culture in Australia revealed a new nostalgia among 16- to 30-year-olds. According to Lifelounge chief executive Dion Appel, nostalgia and simplicity are influencing the styles these young people are adopting, the products they're purchasing and their entertainment choices. Parents' vinyl records are suddenly interesting and vintage clothes are de rigueur, and they want more connections with their tangible, rather than digital friends. They're starting to question the authenticity of social networks such as Facebook and Twitter. They want technology to assist rather than dominate the way they communicate.[51]

Of course you can't touch a digital thing, and people increasingly want to be surrounded by handcrafted stuff. The last few years have seen a resurgence of interest in textile crafts. In a post-feminist world, women have the confidence to reclaim traditional feminine pastimes such as sewing, crafting and quilting and physically making things. But this is no longer seen as limiting the other possibilities of what they can do in the world and therefore diminishing them — it's seen as empowering them.

Indeed knitting has even gone radical, crossing the line from craft to art and now into graffiti. Increasingly it's being used to make political statements. In the city I live in, Wellington, there is a graffiti knitting crew called Outdoor Knit that by night venture out into the streets stitching their knitted art onto telephone poles, fences and street signs. In the United States a group of elderly women calling themselves the Granny Peace Brigade staged a knit-in about a block from the White House and made covers for impaired limbs in protest against the war in Iraq.

Collaboration, and its foundation, trust, will be the style of the next decade. As the internet has evolved, more and more business models founded on collaboration are emerging. Opinions and ideas are shared, filtered and collated to create something new. Today's 20-somethings or 'millennials' are active users of the internet and are not as easily influenced by the traditional media as previous generations, and they are fast becoming the core consumers of luxury brands.

I have recently noticed, reading glossy magazines, that the stick-thin lollypop look — big head, pin-thin body — is out and rounded is in. But of course, curvy women, this is going to be our decade! In times of plenty, the discipline required to limit one's intake of food and maintain a strict exercise regime, thereby showing extreme control of mind over matter, is seen as a good thing. But when times are genuinely tougher, as they now are, pragmatism and practicality, common sense, making do and the values of our grandparents are what are going to see us through, so extreme control over body image and gym and diet obsession are going to look very uncool and self-absorbed. The new decade isn't going to be one where self-righteousness is going to be admired. What *is* going to be admired is people digging deep to support their families and their communities through a difficult period. A few curves on women's bodies are going to look normal and indicate that there are more important things in your life than whether you can fit the jeans you wore 25 years ago.

In terms of organisations, authentic communication will be absolutely critical. Many, if not most of us, have worked in organisations where employees defeat authenticity and reward gameplaying such as putting up budgets that they know they can easily meet, asking for more money than they know they need and going out of their way to make sure that certain taboo subjects are not discussed. The thing about the internet is that there can't be inauthentic information in today's fast-paced, down-to-the-wire situations. Truths ring true and people will not follow inauthentic leaders. The traditional model of CEO leadership, with one person at the top endowed with all the wisdom and legions of followers, has been shown to be wanting and it will be replaced by much more networked organisations. There still does need to be a CEO, but increasingly they'll no longer be seen as god-like in their status, nor will they see themselves that way. Companies such as Zoe Dryden's Second Base, offering leadership development and coaching built on a platform of humility and reflection, will flourish.

At its core, internet economies are about breaking down walls — walls between areas in business and, even more radically, walls between what's inside and outside the company. It was Ed Zander, then president and chief operating officer of Sun Microsystems, who said that www was the new area code of the world.

My time in Telecom also corresponded with another important tipping point. There have always been those not comfortable with the perceived power of large corporations, but the increasing standard of living enjoyed by so many people over the last decade or so meant this has been muted. The scandals at Enron and WorldCom, among others, and the recent global financial crisis have all contributed hugely to an increasing distrust of big business. I believe the global financial crisis in particular has intensified distrust of big business. Previous downturns have probably also increased anti-business sentiment, which moderated when growth resumed, but the magnitude of the problems that have come to light recently suggest that such sentiment will not disappear quickly this time.

John Mackey, the very successful CEO of Whole Foods Market, the world's leading retailer of natural organic foods, posits in his paper 'Conscious Capitalism — Creating a New Paradigm for Business' (2007) that a business model more in touch with our postmodern, information-rich world will become dominant in the twenty-first century. It will be a complex, self-adapted system of interdependent constituencies, rather than totally focused on returns to shareholders. Maximising profits and shareholder value as the sole purpose of business has created unintended negative consequences, and businesses and corporations are increasingly seen as greedy, selfish, evil and in many cases as despoilers of the environment. To survive and succeed, corporations will have to focus more on identifying the comprehensive purposes for which they exist and work harder to satisfy a broader range of constituencies.

There is no doubt that having a deeper, more transcendent purpose is highly energising for many stakeholders, including customers, staff, management and the communities in which a business participates. The trick will be getting investors to see that the investor-focused model will not only be unacceptable, it will also no longer be the best way to drive profits long term.

It is going to take a shift in consciousness in those institutions to establish a new equilibrium. The intermediate phase, the phase I believe we're in now, is going to see clamour for more regulation because of a perceived failure of regulation to deal with many of the unintended consequences of capitalism. A BBC World Service poll released in September 2009 by GlobeScan showed that only 11 per cent of people surveyed across 27 countries thought free market capitalisation was working well. An average of 23 per cent across all nations said capitalism was fatally flawed and a new alternative system was needed, while 51 per cent believed its problems could be solved with more regulation and reform.[52]

But a successful new business paradigm cannot be just about

more and more regulation. That will only leave companies in heavily regulated industries with less and less freedom to move to satisfy real or perceived customer needs.

Chapter twenty-three

women's business

I recently went to a fabric fair in a community hall. It hadn't had much advertising, yet you could hardly move for the number of women there. You can also see this trend in the rise of wearable art and the fusion of the worlds of art and fashion.

We're coming into a woman's time in the world, when women will increasingly step forward in business and in politics. Could Michelle Obama be the next US president after Barack? As Eckhart Tolle pointed out in *A New Earth*, 'Women are seldom as completely absorbed in ego as men and they will drive this next wave.'[53]

As the June 2009 issue of *Women's Wear Daily* magazine reported, sewing parties and the tools for fashion do-it-yourself are becoming more prevalent with the cool set. If you look past traditional titles on the newsstand, you'll find new magazines combining fashion layouts, shopping tips and designer profiles with do-it-yourself tips. For example, the debut issue of a new German magazine called *Cut*

— *Leute machen Kleider* (meaning 'people making clothes') came with pull-out patterns for a double-sided scarf, a pleated messenger bag and a batwing minidress. A 31-year-old called Lucie Schmid started the magazine after learning to sew at a class. The first issue of *Cut* sold out in some of Germany and Switzerland's key book and fashion stores.

Sewing circles are popping up as a way to spark interest and teach the craft, as well as providing a creative outlet and a social network of a more traditional kind. We are going to see more of this intersection that is part frugality, part fashion, part desire to make a unique statement, part a reclaiming by women of things that have traditionally been valued by previous generations. My mother is a gifted creator with textiles and I treasure some of the beautiful pieces I wear, I use, I have in my home that she's made for me. For me these objects are intrinsically tied up with the quality of her mothering, which was always very loving. This valuing of personally crafted items will intersect with the online world to create, for example, web-based craft fairs. The internet already abounds with blogs and online communities for knitters and the knitting community also has its own equivalent of Facebook called ravelry.com. There will also be an intersection with design blogs.

Fashion has had a love affair with vintage for several years now. The current market's focus on sustainable products is going to mingle with the undercurrent of nostalgia which has been bubbling away for a while and is only going to increase. But it is going to come around this time in much more of a co-creative dialogue between what has been before and what's possible in a digital world.

I've long talked about California as a place where new trends emerge. And there I was in San Francisco in October 2009, wandering in a square I'd never been to before, and I saw it — a gallery with an exhibition called 'Open Source Embroidery'. Open source embroidery? The exhibition at the Museum of Craft and Folk Art brought together software programmers, HTML users and craftspeople to share their skills and create works of art together, with names such as 'HTML Patchwork' and 'HTML Embroideries'. Some of my friends had thought I was nuts when I'd said not long before this that I thought the re-embracing of traditional female art and craft would come back in some different form as a product of the digital age that we're all part of. And here it was before my very eyes — a complete integration of artworks using embroidery threads and computer code.

But it's not just about clothes and crafts. We women need to be bold, have a dream. Having a dream or a goal means that you can focus and make choices that take you closer to how you want to live your life.

We all want to master something that is important to us and be recognised for it. I knew from the age of 17 that I wanted to make a career in the corporate world and run a large public company before I was 40. That knowledge helped me choose my degrees and shaped my career choices, for example when I took that sideways step from Television New Zealand to National Mutual to extend my skills and open up new opportunities.

There's something in the New Zealand psyche, a 'give it a go' mentality, that has helped me and other women fulfil our ambitions. There is also an egalitarian streak that runs through New Zealand society which means there is less to stop women aiming for the top than in many other countries.

Nevertheless, even though there are fewer obstacles, that does not mean there are none, and while blatant displays of sexism are unusual in corporate New Zealand, there are often subtle barriers to advancement. Informal discrimination against women still exists and there is a lot of unconscious and systemic sexism which works to block women's advancement. While we shouldn't be surprised by sexism when we encounter it, nor should we accept it in any way. Find a way through, over, under or around it. I also think that because we experience discrimination as women we should be acutely aware of other types of discrimination — race, age and so on — and work to end it.

I am a firm believer that women need to support other women. It is important that we help and encourage each other to be successful, by mentoring or assisting women to retrain or re-enter the workforce, and in any other ways we can.

I think women are often held back at a deeply subconscious level. We expect that our good work will be recognised and rewarded and our leadership qualities noted and encouraged by those around us, but this is often not the case. Even women who have strong business leadership experience often focus so much of their energy on the particular institution they are part of that they don't think to nurture their networks and plan for the next step in the way that many men do. For example, I think I made a mistake by not joining a corporate board while I was CEO at Telecom. It would have provided a very useful bridge to other opportunities upon leaving the company. I didn't do so early on because I felt completely occupied with the challenge in front of me, then in the middle years I was too focused on whether the Telecom board would approve of such a move, and in the final couple of years I was again engulfed in too much drama to make it a real possibility. However, I realise now that I had my opportunities and I should have seized them with both hands at the time.

One of the most important benefits of the internet revolution is that it values qualities of creativity, innovation and lateral thinking, and fosters behaviours of partnership, collaboration and cooperation. These tend to be more female qualities and behaviours than male ones. Women's nurturing sensibilities become a very powerful tool for holding disparate people together over a network. The most effective managers and the most creative people transcend sexual stereotypes in their capacity to be both receptive nurturers and active and assertive. Give yourself permission to express the most appropriate behaviour in any situation you find yourself in.

Discovering what your dream is is probably the most important thing you can do but is also one of the most difficult. You can't force it but you do need to keep working at it — defining and refining it.

Many people spend more time planning their holidays than they do planning their dream!

Some of us are blessed by knowing at a young age that we have an outstanding talent and passion for, say, music or dance or mathematics, but for many of us it's a matter of setting aside time to be honest and reflect on what we have in our life that we want more of. What do we have that needs to be released because it's no longer serving us? What do we not have in our life that we want? Tertiary education can be great for opening yourself up to new possibilities and directions, as can travel.

Once you know what your dream is, find yourself some role models. These are the people who are going to keep you inspired to follow that dream. They don't have to be women, although if you're working in an area that is non-traditional for women, having female role models and mentors can be a real advantage in plotting your way around obstacles. They don't necessarily have to be people you know. When she was a young Australian-Aboriginal girl dreaming of being the world's fastest female runner, the Olympian Cathy Freeman kept posters of Raelene Boyle, another Aussie who was a world-champion sprinter, on her bedroom wall. I am also proud of being a role model myself. After I spoke at a Telecom-sponsored women's convention at Queen's Birthday Weekend in 2005, organiser Margaret Shields wrote to me to say that 30 years ago it would have been almost impossible to imagine having a woman in my position in New Zealand. My active presence in the business world showed that it was possible for women to do anything.

Ever since I decided that I wanted to get to the top in business I kept clippings from newspapers and magazines about other businesswomen and their success. I also own just about every book ever written on the subject of women in management: *Women Leading, A Chance for the Top, Breaking into the Boardroom, Self-Confidence Trick, Success for Women, The Female Advantage, The New Executive Woman, The Women's Way to the Top*. I devoured these books for ideas that I could use to advance my career. And these days you don't have to restrict yourself to books — go on the web and you will find huge amounts of material written by women for women who want to be in business leadership roles. At the end of the day, though, you do have to do it yourself. No one else can do it for you.

Be your dream in your mind and your heart. Do what's required to achieve that dream and then enjoy having it.

We're all afraid at different times, even if some of us do a better job of hiding it than others. From time to time, you're allowed a rest in your commitment to whatever challenge you have taken on. You're allowed an occasional weep but you must press on. You need to face any fear squarely and conquer it. An uncertain, apprehensive person will not make a success of anything. No one else will have confidence in you unless you have confidence in yourself, so even if you're uncertain or afraid about a decision, once you've made it, execute it with confidence. The worst that can happen is that you will be proved wrong and will have to remedy the situation, but that's much better than not having tried at all.

At the end of the day, attitude leads your behaviour. I firmly believe that you make yourself with your disposition. In my observation, success in business and life is based more on mental attitude than mental capability. Often people who appear more successful haven't actually had an easier life, they have just more persistently and consistently controlled their perspective about things.

It is important is to look after yourself. It seems so obvious, but you do need to look after your health if you're going to operate at your peak physically, mentally and emotionally. As I've explained, when I was in my mid-twenties and had just started working at National Mutual while still completing my law degree, I got very stressed. That stress presented itself in a lot of health-related issues such as back problems and problems with my teeth, so I had to find ways of dealing with it. I created a number of habits to reduce stress which are still part of my life: daily swims, a weekly massage and drinking alcohol only occasionally. Swimming is a cross between exercise and meditation for me. It's not full-on, heart-thumping exercise but it's refreshing, gives me time to think and is my transition into the day. And horse riding also brings me relaxation and enjoyment.

Above all, take responsibility for your own life. You can't change the past, you can't change people around you, but you can be your best self. Every day you can start anew, vowing to live that day as your best self.

There is much we can do to ensure more women have the opportunity to fulfil their potential, but the existence of opportunity does not guarantee success. Getting to the top in business still takes focus, determination and hard work. There are times when you might work to the point of exhaustion. The fact is it's difficult to lead a balanced life when you're leading a company — you have to be so relentless, so focused, so onto everything that it's hard not to exclude some other things from your life.

As a woman, I believe you can have it all — just not necessarily all at the same time. John and I never married, a situation we were both completely at ease with and that never caused any angst between us. For my part, I was such a strong feminist that I couldn't get past the history of women's unequal relationship to men in the institution of marriage. I just did not want to be someone's wife. For John's part, he was never a 'joining the institution' sort of a person either. I think John regarded marriage as a bit like an emotional union that was recognised by the police. Similarly, neither of us ever wanted children — me because I knew I didn't have the resilience and tolerance for the sleep deprivation that it would involve, plus I knew I couldn't get to the top in my career *and* have children, and in John's case, because of his need for long periods of solitude to pursue his artistic gifts. But even if we had had children, we would not have got married.

It is important to aim for self-knowledge and honesty, particularly about your own strengths and weaknesses, and to use this knowledge to help you set goals and ask for advice. Most women come to the realisation that they don't know it all, and can't do everything by themselves, a realisation that's often easier for women to admit than men. I am quite open to people giving me advice about what we should do and how we should do it, and I've tried to make this openness a central component of my leadership style.

I, like many women, don't support the John Wayne model of leadership, where a lone figure rides into town, figures out what the problems are and rides off again, leaving everyone living happily ever after. The only thing that appeals to me about that is the horse riding! I am a team-oriented person and I believe getting the right leadership team in place is possibly the most important thing a leader can do. I look for team members with intelligence, high aspirations and a focus on excellence and I expect them to subordinate their own egos for the good of the whole and to value and trust their fellow team members.

I used to think that leadership was about personality and, as an extrovert myself, tended to have a picture in my head of leaders as extroverts. I learnt over a period of years that leadership has nothing to do with personality and everything to do with *character*. A good leader knows it's important to have the humility to ask for and listen to feedback. It's important to understand that no situation is sustainable unless everybody's pieces of the jigsaw puzzle fit together.

Different styles work for different people. Some are more formal in their leadership and operating style, others are more inspirational, heart-level leaders. A great leader creates a space that allows for other people's expression of their own personality and to develop other great leaders but this needs to be wrapped around the common goals, values and purpose of the organisation.

It is important to be the best that you can be in your current role while always having other long-term goals to inspire your personal development. It's a state of mind that's equally applicable to women starting their career or in their first management position or when they've become CEO. It's a state of mind that honours the achievements of the early generations of women who struggled for our right to pursue our dreams.

During my lifetime there has been a profound shift. The most recognised women in the world may be singers and movie stars rather than bank CEOs, entrepreneurs and media moguls, but girls now think that they can do anything. However, it is a real risk thinking that equal opportunity is ancient history and that the workforce is a more or less level playing field for both sexes. Women are still thinly planted on the executive landscape, although some people still believe it's just a matter of time before the power of positive thinking translates into economic power. In my experience women are still being told they are too strong, too forthright to be CEOs — 'criticisms' that would never be directed at a man. Indeed, just a few months ago I was approached by a headhunter asking me if I was interested in putting myself forward for the role of CEO of a very large company. Although not necessarily looking to be a CEO again, as I was perfectly happy with my various ventures, including the writing of this book, I indicated that I was interested in this particular opportunity. After many weeks I had heard nothing and then finally she rang me back to say that the chair of this organisation, after conferring with a few of the board members, did not wish to take the conversation with me any further. She said he thought I was 'a very strong, a very driven, a very forthright person, altogether too strong a personality'. 'It's a style thing,' the chair had said. 'I just don't know if I can work with her.'

Given my extensive background in banking and telecommunications, the two industries most relevant to this enterprise, there would have been no possibility of saying that I wasn't suitably qualified or experienced, so it had to be a style thing, didn't it? I was gobsmacked. While no CEO appointment is ever predictable, as it is always at least partly about context and timing and there are usually several strong candidates, it had never occurred to me that if I expressed a serious interest in the role the board wouldn't want to meet with me. As it happened, I was at a social function with this particular chair a few days later and I asked to discuss it with him. To his credit, he met with me — not that that shone any further light on the situation.

When I recounted what happened to a male friend, he looked at me incredulously and said, 'It's almost unbelievable, that having got to the top of Telecom, an even larger company than this one, and been the CEO for so many years, that that could happen to you, Theresa. If it could happen to you, it could happen to any woman.' Precisely. It can, and it does.

The education system is probably the institutional setting that is the most supportive of equality between the genders. After all, male and female students count equally in terms of numbers, which institutions often rely on to get funding, and the system for 'winning', or at least winning approval, is straightforward: getting as high a score as possible. The transition to the real world can sometimes be difficult for women when they discover winning, and winning approval, is no longer so straightforward.

I grew up in a family where cleverness was prized more than femininity and I was well into my thirties before I consciously thought about the need to balance my male and female energies. Girls, wrote Kathy Esson in a wonderful piece in *The Bulletin* in September 2000 called 'The Venus Trap',[54] are simultaneously socialised into two ways of being in the world: a female way and a male way. At its best this makes them extraordinarily good operators, combining sensitivity to others with very strong competence and belief in themselves.

Women's achievements should not be taken for granted or read as inviolate, and that is well illustrated in New Zealand. In 2001 Helen Clark was the Prime Minister; Jenny Shipley, a former Prime Minister, was Leader of the Opposition; Sian Elias was the Chief Justice; Margaret Wilson was the Attorney-General; Christine Fletcher was the mayor of Auckland, the largest city in New Zealand; Jeanette Fitzsimons was the co-leader of the Green Party; Silvia Cartwright was Governor-General; and I was the chief executive of Telecom, the largest listed company in New Zealand. At the New Zealand Women's Convention in June 2005 Silvia Cartwright, who was a keynote speaker, observed that she'd be very surprised if in due course people like herself, me and Helen Clark were replaced by other women. History was to prove her right. At the time of writing in 2009, there is a male Prime Minister, a male Leader of the Opposition, a male Attorney-General, a male mayor of Auckland, a male Governor-General and a male CEO of Telecom. I am pleased to report that there is still a female co-leader of the Green Party and Sian Elias is still the Chief Justice!

I wish I'd known at 25 that life is a really long time and you don't need to be in such a hurry. I never took the time to travel outside my business trips. I wish I'd been more spontaneous. I lived an extremely focused life, like an athlete, focused on goals, discipline and stamina, and suddenly, in my mid-forties, that was gone. I had no idea how to create the next opportunity, something I'd never felt in my life before, but which has given me greater empathy for how many other women feel.

After I got used to being able to take my time to do things I enjoyed, do them more often, do them more slowly and live a more flexible life, I began to feel a different sort of being-in-flow from that which I'd enjoyed during much of my time as CEO; a more peaceful, relaxed centeredness, with less anxiety about what that day, or the next day, or the next week, might bring. But of course that was only possible with financial independence, which was in turn made possible by having a high-paying position for many years, and I am grateful for that.

As immigrants from a very modest background, one of my parents', and particularly my father's, early lessons was the need for his daughters to be financially independent. I knew at any early age that you couldn't rely financially on a man — you could get divorced, he could be dumped from his job or get sick — rely on the state or even rely on your wider family. You needed to be able to do it for yourself. I still believe that it is important for every human being to know that they can financially support themselves.

I always wanted to live a self-determined life. I am not interested in controlling people, just controlling my own destiny. It's very satisfying to achieve what you have been striving for, but you must make sure to actually enjoy the journey on the way up. You might never get to the top and if you don't enjoy what you're doing along the way, your working life isn't going to be all that satisfying. You mustn't take roles just because you think they are a means to an end. I was told I could never be a CEO if I stayed on the marketing track, but I didn't want to work in general administration so I stayed in marketing and still became a CEO.

So what of feminism? Naomi Woolf has written very recently that maybe Western women's role in defining feminism is over, in favour of passing the torch to women from other cultures in the East.[55] She points out that their agenda is more pressing and their problems more serious. In the West, the counterpoint to women as property has been a highly individualistic demand for personal autonomy, and decision-making based primarily on a woman's own wishes rather than as wife, mother, community member or worshipper. The core theory with which emerging feminists from more traditional, religious societies are working is different from Western feminism and in some ways is more profound and humane. In India, for example, feminists have articulated a vision of equality that is family-centred rather than self-centred and values service to community rather than personal gratification. This vision of feminism is based on the notion that women can claim equality yet still have a valued role in the home, putting women's rights in the context of community and spirituality. Maybe this is a development of Western feminism rather than a reduction of its powers, but it's hard to tell.

On the real frontline of feminism, to challenge male power as a woman is still to invite death. In 2005, at the age of 27, Malalai Joya became Afghanistan's youngest MP. Running for Parliament as an independent, she romped in as women flocked to vote for her. 'The very first time I spoke in parliament my microphone was cut off, a practice I've become accustomed to,' she wrote in her memoir, *Raising My Voice*. 'My days in parliament were always stressful and lonely because I was constantly being attacked and insulted.' In May 2006, after she had made another abbreviated speech about rape, the parliament went into uproar. 'I had to duck behind my desk as they hurled water bottles at me and sandals flew over my head.'

A year later, after refusing to apologise for comparing the Afghan parliament to a zoo, she was suspended for the rest of her five-year term by the vote of a parliamentary majority. In July this year, *The Dominion-Post* reported that no action has been taken against the members of the same body who had called her a whore and threatened her with death.[56]

With 80 per cent female illiteracy, conditions in Afghanistan for women remain abysmal. During the nineteenth century the paramount moral challenge was slavery. In the twentieth century it was totalitarianism. In this century it is the brutality inflicted on so many women and girls around the globe — sex crimes and other physical abuse, human trafficking, acid attacks, bride burnings and mass rape. Pulitzer Prize winning journalists Nicholas Kristof and Sheryl WuDunn have written about this extensively. In a large slice of the world girls are uneducated and women marginalised and it is not an accident that these same countries are disproportionately mired in poverty and driven by fundamentalism and chaos. There's a growing recognition among everyone from the World Bank to the US military joint chiefs of staff to aid organisations such as CARE that focusing on women and girls is the most effective way to fight poverty and extremism. That's why foreign aid is increasingly directed to women.

If you live in America, the phrase 'gender discrimination' might conjure thoughts of unequal pay, underfinanced sports teams or unwanted touching from a boss. In the developing world, meanwhile, millions of women and girls are actually enslaved. The International Labour Organization estimates that at any one time there are 12.3 million people engaged in forced labour of all kinds, including sexual servitude. Children working in the sex trade are held in conditions indistinguishable from slavery, according to a UN report. Girls and women are locked in brothels and beaten if they resist, fed just enough to be kept alive and often sedated with drugs.

The global statistics on the abuse of girls are numbing. It appears that more girls and women are now missing from the planet, precisely because they are female, than men were killed on the battlefield in all the wars of the twentieth century. The number of victims of this routine 'gendercide' far exceeds the number of people who were slaughtered in all the genocides of that same period.

For many poor countries, the greatest unexploited resource isn't oilfields or gold: it's the women and girls who aren't educated and have never become a major presence in the formal economy. With education and help starting businesses, impoverished women can earn money and support their country as well as their families. They represent perhaps the best hope for fighting global poverty.[57]

Investment in girls' education may well be the most valuable investment in the developing world, Larry Summers wrote when he was chief economist of the World Bank. Goldman Sachs concluded in a 2008 research report that gender inequality hurts economic growth, and emphasised how much developing countries could improve their current performance by educating girls. Policymakers are getting the message: President Obama has appointed a new White House Council for Women and Girls, with Secretary of State Hillary Clinton as a member, and has set up a new state department office of global women's issues. At her confirmation hearing, Clinton said that she would put women's issues at the core of American foreign policy. As Clare Lockhart, a former UN adviser to the Afghan government, has pointed out, the real way you get societal shift is when women have economic rights and assets.[58]

Feminism has become something of a dirty word in the West, particularly among women in the corporate suite, but if it gets to the point where there are no feminists, we will wake up one day and find a lot of opportunities for women are shutting down. One of my concerns about young women coming through now is that they don't necessarily appreciate what other women before them have done to lay the groundwork for their own success. I feel quite keenly that the life I enjoy is possible because other women fought for the right to go to university and the right to vote. These things are not enjoyed by all women today and should not be taken for granted.

History is not necessarily a straight line. It can easily be a cycle. It's important for women to honour what's been created by people who've gone before them — men and women — and to make sure those lessons of history are not lost.

Chapter twenty-four

coming
full circle

It was weird, truly it was. Not long after I'd signed the contract with Random House to write this book, and only a few days into the writing of it, I took a break to walk down to my local bookshop, as I had just started to realise the enormity of the project I'd taken on. I happened to pick up a copy of that month's *Unlimited* magazine and my eye was immediately drawn to an article: 'The Write Stuff — Should Business Figures Publish Autobiographical Handbooks?' In that article Bob Wallace, a person whom to the best of my knowledge I have never met, was quoted as saying that a book by Graham Hart about his life in business would sell like hot cakes, and the same went for Stephen Tindall, Ralph Norris, Theresa Gattung and Sam Morgan. 'I would say there's probably a book in each of them, but I guess they have to feel the need or be driven to do it. In many respects entrepreneurs are people more oriented towards doing things and writing a book takes an awful lot of focus. It's about setting time aside.' Indeed!

In February 2009 I was very proud to be named one of the top 10 New Zealand business figures of the past decade.[59] I feel really proud of my time at Telecom. When I joined the company no one had heard of the internet and hardly anyone had a mobile phone. My dozen years there in leadership roles and ultimately as CEO coincided with an unprecedented time of change.

Of course, knowing what I know now, I would have done some things differently. In particular I think we should have introduced more game-breaking moves for customers like $5 talk-as-long-as-you-like calling, and $10 'all-you-can-eat' texting, moves which changed the way people used telecommunications services. And I think we focused for too long on the conversion from dial-up internet to broadband and getting basic broadband out as far as possible and should have shifted the focus sooner to the urban, high-value, high-user customer group. But my job was to deliver for shareholders, and in the five years to the end of 2007, Telecom New Zealand was the second highest creator of value for shareholders in New Zealand (after Fletcher Building).[60]

I was the only woman on that list of the top 10 business figures in New Zealand in the last decade. I am still the only woman to have headed a major listed company in New Zealand and I'm now one of the few women in this country to chair a company that is not family owned.

I believe it is still harder for women to get to the top than it is for men. It's harder to become CEO and to be seen as a leader. I think the image of a CEO is still of a hard-driving male. Being a CEO is a challenging, stimulating, fantastic but tough job for anybody. I don't think the criteria for being a CEO is different for men or women. I do, however, think the margins of error are smaller for women in leadership positions.

I never would have believed, growing up in Rotorua, that I would have made the *Forbes* list of the world's 50 most powerful women. I've met great leaders of state and some of the richest people in the world, and I've worked with volunteers who earn nothing. I've experienced incredible physical pain with my TMJ problems in my twenties, my back problems in my thirties and my falls from moving objects (horses) or being hit by them (a car). At times I have been so stressed that my periods have stopped and my eyelids have flickered involuntarily.

I was brought up to treat the truth as non-negotiable. I've learnt the hard way that not everyone else does. I've experienced the exhilaration of success and the loneliness of defeat. I've experienced people betraying me and people sacrificing much for me. I've experienced tremendous love and support from family, friends and colleagues and the kindness of strangers. I've learnt that everything counts — big things and small things — because they might be small to you, but they can be very significant to someone else. I've learnt that it's about as useful to put people in boxes — people who work for a charity are good, businesspeople are bad — as it is to decide that you're only going to wear green clothes on a Monday and blue clothes on a Tuesday.

It takes focus and dedication to excel. In particular I'm unreconstructed in my view that a woman must be able to support herself financially, and that women cannot have equal status in their society unless they have economic power. I've come to see that my life has for the most part been very outwardly directed, with me sitting largely in my male energy, the energy of leadership, in a world which values logic and outcome and achievement and results.

But since leaving Telecom I've rediscovered the simple joys of life: of waking up when I want instead of when the alarm clock goes off; of spending time with a good friend without half an eye on the clock; the joy of pets and what animals can teach us about living in the moment — witness a cat's simple enjoyment of stretching out in the sunshine. I see that I am a better balanced person now, that I'm not singularly focused on my next goal. Female energy is not better than male energy, of course, but I believe they need to be brought into balance in each of us and in the world. And, I've started riding over jumps again!

Endnotes

1 *Wool — A History of New Zealand's Wool Industry*, Bill Carter & John MacGibbon, Ngaio Press, 2003

2 'Feminism — the sequel', *The Listener*, July 17, 2004

3 *Managing Your Brilliant Career — a Guide for Women in Management*, Helen Place, Motivation Inc., 1982

4 *Campaign Brief*, December 1993

5 *Evening Post*, May 15, 1999

6 Infotech Comment, Adrienne Perry, *Dominion Infotech Weekly*, Issue no. 406

7 *The Independent*, October 13, 1999

8 *Evening Post*, July 22, 2000; *Sunday Star-Times*, July 16, 2000

9 *Evening Post*, February 24, 2000

10 *New Zealand Herald*, March 25, 2002

11 *The Australian*, April 17, 2002

12 *The Independent*, April 10, 2002

13 *The Dominion-Post*, July 15, 2002

14 *National Business Review*, November 8, 2002

15 *National Business Review*, November 8, 2002

16 *Australian Financial Review*, August 6, 2003

17 *Sunday Star-Times*, December 14, 2003

18 Deutsche Bank research note on Telecom NZ reported in *The Australian Financial Review*, January 21, 2004

19 *New Zealand Herald*, July 13, 2004

20 *Australian Financial Review*, March 22, 2004; *The Dominion-Post*, August 2, 2004

21 *Australian Financial Review*, August 6, 2004

22 *New Zealand Herald*, May 4, 2006

23 *National Business Review*, February 3, 2006

24 *New Zealand Herald*, February 4, 2006

25 New Zealand Infotech, *The Dominion-Post*, March 20, 2006

26 *Sunday Star-Times*, February 19, 2006

27 *Herald on Sunday*, June 11, 2006

28 *The Independent*, June 14, 2006

29 *New Zealand Herald*, August 8, 2006

30 *The Dominion-Post*, August 21, 2006

31 *New Zealand Herald*, November 4, 2009

32 *National Business Review*, November 6, 2009

33 *The Dominion-Post*, June 1, 2007

34 *The Dominion-Post*, November 29, 2006

35 *Weekend Herald*, February 2/3, 2002

36 Chanticleer, *Australian Financial Review*, May 2009

37 *The Listener*, May 2, 2009

38 *Whose High Country?*, Roberta McIntyre, Penguin, 2008

39 *Australian Financial Review*, September 16, 2009

40 *Australian Financial Review*, September 16, 2009

41 *Australian Financial Review*, October 15, 2009

42 *The Independent*, October 22, 2009

43 *The Dominion-Post*, October 22, 2009

44 *The Independent*, September 10, 2009

45 *Melbourne Age*, August 19, 2009

46 see Geering L, *God, Gaia and Us: Moving Towards a New Form of Mysticism*, The St Andrew's Trust for the Study of Religion and Society, 2008; Tolle E, *A New Earth: Awakening to your Life's Purpose*, Plume, 2006

47 Escape, *Sunday Star-Times*, November 22, 2009

48 Schwartz, B, 'The real crisis: we stopped being wise', TEO talks, 2009 http://www.ted.com/index.php/talks/barry_schwartz_on_on_loss_of_wisdom.html.

49 Lord Patten from an address he gave to New Zealand business leaders in Auckland, New Zealand at the end of 2008

50 *New Zealand Herald*, August 8, 2009

51 *New Zealand Herald*, July 17, 2009 (from *The Australian*)

52 *The Dominion-Post*, September 10, 2009

53 Tolle E, *A New Earth: Awakening to your Life's Purpose*, Plume, 2006

54 'The Venus Trap', *The Bulletin*, September 2000

55 *The Dominion-Post*, May 5, 2009

56 *The Dominion-Post*, July 18, 2009

57 Kristof, Nicholas D and WuDunn, Sheryl, in an essay in the *New York Times*, August 23, 2009, adapted from their book *Half The Sky — Turning Oppression into Opportunity for Women Worldwide*, Random House, 2009

58 *The Dominion-Post*, August 6, 2009

59 *New Zealand Herald*, February 10, 2009

60 Boston Consulting Group Report, *New Zealand Herald*, July 2, 2008